MOVIE CROSSWORD PUZZLES

DYLANNA PRESS

Published by Dylanna Press an imprint of Dylanna Publishing, Inc.
Copyright © 2022 by Dylanna Press

All rights reserved. No part of this publication may be reproduced, stored in a retrieval system, or transmitted by any means, including electronic, mechanical, photocopying, or otherwise, without prior written permission of the publisher.

Limit of liability/Disclaimer of Warranty: The Publisher and the author make no representations or warranties with respect to the accuracy or completeness of the contents of this work and specifically disclaim all warranties, including without limitation warranties of fitness for a particular purpose.

Although the publisher has taken all reasonable care in the preparation of this book, we make no warranty about the accuracy or completeness of its content and, to the maximum extent permitted, disclaim all liability arising from its use.

Trademarks: Dylanna Press is a registered trademark of Dylanna Publishing, Inc. and may not be used without written permission.

#1

Across

3. Film movement popular in France in 1950s (3,4)
5. Ray Liotta, Unlawful ____ (5)
6. The Seventh ____ (4)
10. You Don't Mess with the _____ (5)
12. Zoolander fashion line (9)
13. Wreck-It _____, animated (5)
14. Won best actress in 2007 for La Vie en Rose (6,9)
17. Plays Mr. Blonde in Reservoir Dogs (7,6)
19. My Fair ____ (4)
20. "I love the smell of _____ in the morning" (6)
21. Triangle of ____ (7)
24. Won best actress in 1965 for Darling, Julie ____ (8)
25. Dancer in the _____ (4)
26. Corleone family is part of ____ (5)
27. DiCaprio on island (7,6)
28. In the Heat of the _____ (5)
32. "I'm walkin' _____" (4)
34. For a Few Dollars ____ (4)
35. For Your Eyes _____ (4)
36. Die Hard director, John (9)
37. Star of Dances with Wolves (7)

Down

1. Maggie _____, brother is also an actor (10)
2. 1st movie to show a toilet flushing (6)
4. Harry Potter is a ____ (6)
5. Terms of ____ (10)
7. Highest grossing movie 2014, directed by Eastwood (8,6)
8. Won best actor in 1991 for The Silence of the Lambs (7,7)
9. Jack Nicholson navy movie (3,4,6)
11. Sam Raimi, Drag Me to ____ (4)
15. Won best actress in 2019 for Judy (5,9)
16. Jennifer Beals dancing movie (10)
18. Christian Bale, Malick, Knight of ____ (4)
22. 8 Mile is about life of (6)
23. The actors in a film (4)
24. Brad Pitt, Fight _____ (4)
29. Mean _____, high school (5)
30. 1948 Hitchcock, you can tie things with this (4)
31. Eyes Without a ____ (4)
33. Confessions of a Dangerous _____ (4)

#2

Across

1. The last movie Tony Scott directed, train (11)
4. Willy Wonka, Augustus _____ (5)
10. The Man From _____ (5)
11. From the moment they met it was murder. (6,9)
14. Person with artistic control over film (8)
15. Daily filming schedule (4,5)
17. Boxing movie (5)
18. Number of Toy Story movies (4)
19. On Golden _____ (4)
21. Harrison Ford's character in The Fugitive (7,6)
23. Highest grossing movie of 1974, Mel Brooks (7,7)
25. Death on the _____ (4)
27. Clooney, Jennifer Lopez, bank robbery (3,2,5)
29. MLK biopic 2014 (5)
30. "Don" (9)
31. The Evil _____ (4)
32. Gone Baby _____ (4)
33. Director of Pearl (2,4)

Down

2. Batman (1989) director (3,6)
3. Won best actor in 1949 All the King's Men (9,8)
5. Jurassic _____ (4)
6. Last Night in _____ (4)
7. Director of Get Out (6,5)
8. The Lion in the _____, season (6)
9. Notting _____ (4)
10. The Hills Have _____ (4)
12. The Fighter based on real life of (5,4)
13. A follow-up film (6)
16. Won best actor in 1988 for Rain Man (7)
20. Postcards from the _____ (4)
21. Spike Lee, Do the _____ (5,5)
22. David Lynch 1980, The _____ Man (8)
24. Will Smith, I Am _____ (6)
26. Country of Call Me By Your Name (5)
27. A Clockwork _____ (6)
28. Jordan Peele 2022 movie (4)
29. The Truman _____ (4)

#3

Across

1. The Empire _____ (7,4)
6. Scorsese animated movie (4)
8. Gangster movie, Sexy _____ (5)
9. Dan Akroyd and Eddie Murphy (7,6)
11. What they travel through in Interstellar (8)
12. Top Gun sequel (8)
15. Won best actress in in 1975 for One Flew Over the Cuckoo's Nest (6,8)
18. Movie about stock traders, Boiler _____ (4)
19. Tom Cruise and Jamie Foxx, LA cab driver (10)
21. Jeff Bridges, The Big _____ (8)
23. "You're gonna need a bigger…." (4)
26. Blood _____, Coen (6)
28. Shrek, Lord _____ (8)
31. "Greed, for lack of a better word, is _____" (4)
33. Before the Devil Knows _____ (5,4)
34. Assassin who takes in 12-year-old girl (4)
35. The Blair Witch project set in (8)

Down

2. The Polar Express is going to (3,5,4)
3. Edward Norton suffers from _____ in Fight Club (8)
4. Javier _____ (6)
5. Voice of Anna in Frozen (7,4)
6. Cusack, record store owner (4,8)
7. Pride & ____ (9)
10. Director of Boyhood (9)
13. High schooler writes about a band for Rolling Stone magazine (6,6)
14. Fashion, House of _____ (5)
16. Bruce Banner (4)
17. Fiddler on the ____ (4)
20. Won best actor for The Revenant, _____ DiCaprio (8)
22. Halle ____ (5)
24. Gone with the _____ (4)
25. Born on the Fourth _____ (2,4)
27. The Devil Wears ____ (5)
29. Zoolander first name (5)
30. Child of Deaf adults (4)
31. The Imitation _____, Cumberbatch (4)
32. The Blind ____ (4)

#4

Across

4. Field of _____ (6)
7. Bad guy in Dirty Harry (7,6)
11. Home _____, Reese Witherspoon (5)
12. Won best actress in 1962 for The Miracle Worker (4,8)
14. "I want to be _____" (5)
15. Star of Back to the Future (7,1,3)
20. Ingrid Goes _____ (4)
22. Forrest Gump's ping pong team travels here (5)
23. Animated town known for its irreverence (5,4)
24. Less Than _____, Downey Jr. (4)
25. Played Mark Zuckerberg (5,9)
29. Bad roommate, Single White _____ (6)
31. "Escape or die frying." (7,3)
34. CODA is about ____ people (4)
36. Daniel Day ____ (5)
37. Magazine in Almost Famous (7,5)
38. Eastwood, Pale _____ (5)
39. _____ Pierce (7)

Down

1. A _____ Tale, De Niro (5)
2. The Aviator is about (6,6)
3. The Last Days of _____ (5)
5. Saving Private _____ (4)
6. "Mrs. Robinson, you're trying to _____ me" (6)
8. Horror director, Wes ____ (6)
9. The Professional (4)
10. Animated, rat in the kitchen (11)
13. Won best actor in 1950 for Cyrano de Bergerac (4,6)
16. 1963, The Great ____ (6)
17. Plays the Joker in Tim Burton's Batman (4,9)
18. Ian McKellen Lord of the Rings character (7)
19. The Sound of _____ (5)
21. Brad Pitt plays ancient warrior (4)
26. East of _____ (4)
27. Ferris (7)
28. Wooly mammoth in Ice Age (7)
30. "No wire hangers, ____" (4)
32. Rooney Mara and Cate Blanchett 1950s romance (5)
33. ___ Fonda (4)
35. Sunset ___ (4)

#5

Across

6. Won best actress in 2009 for The Blind Side (6,7)
9. Non-Jedi who can use a lightsaber (3,4)
10. Glengarry Glen Ross writer/director (5,5)
11. Bohemian _____ (8)
12. Park Chan-wook 2003 movie (6)
15. James Bond goes into space (9)
17. Witherspoon (5)
19. Raging Bull is about a (5)
20. Patrick Bateman (9,4)
22. The Social Network college (7)
24. Winter's Bone star (8)
25. The Philadelphia _____ (5)
27. "Love means never having to say you're _____" (5)
29. Bambi's friend the skunk (6)
31. The Iron _____ (5)
33. Michael Douglas and Sharon Stone (5,8)
34. The Lincoln _____ (6)
35. Simba's father (6)

Down

1. Tár (4,9)
2. Plays Mr. White in Reservoir Dogs (6,6)
3. Dial M for _____ (6)
4. Dustin Hoffman adopts a female alter ego (7)
5. 2022 Marilyn Monroe movie (6)
7. Won best actress in 1987 for Moonstruck (4)
8. Won a record 4 Oscars for best actress (9,7)
13. Dead but life of party (6)
14. Portrayed Karen Hill character in Goodfellas (8,6)
16. Won best actor in 1964 for My Fair Lady (3,8)
18. The Long Good _____ (6)
21. North by _____, Hitchock (9)
23. 2021 Aretha Franklin biopic (7)
25. Where the Crawdads ___ (4)
26. Boat in Jaws (4)
28. The Breakfast _____ (4)
30. Minor actor in crowd scenes (5)
32. Taste of Cherry country (4)

#6

Across

1. Requiem for a _____ (5)
3. Godfather Part II Michael travels to here on New Years eve (4)
5. Hostages in Iran, Affleck (4)
11. Won best actress in 1956 for Anastasia (6,7)
14. Voices Dory in Finding Nemo (5)
15. Ace Ventura: _____ (3,9)
17. Won best actor in 1943 Watch on the Rhine (4,5)
19. Angelina Jolie witch movie (10)
23. Pacino is a cop, De Niro is a robber (4)
24. 1997, Life Is _____ (9)
25. 28 Days _____ (5)
26. "You can't handle the ____!" (5)
28. Stanley Kubrick's final film (4,4,4)
30. From Dusk Till _____ (4)
32. Grosse Pointe _____ (5)
33. Star of 1954 Sabrina (6,7)
34. Willem (5)
35. Michael Fassbender plays a sex addict (5)

Down

2. A daytime show (7)
3. The Da Vinci _____ (4)
4. Kiss Kiss Bang _____ (4)
6. Beauty and the _____ (5)
7. Sandra _____ (7)
8. Won best actor in 1985 for Kiss of the Spider Woman (7,4)
9. Highest grossing movie of 1984, Eddie Murphy (7,5,3)
10. Spike Lee favorite sports team (6)
12. Thing they're searching for in Stand by Me (4)
13. Highest grossing movie of 1983, Star Wars (6,2,3,4)
16. Star of The Fly, Jeff _____ (8)
18. _____ Named Desire (1,9)
20. Earlier event (9)
21. Rosebud (7,4)
22. Costner, minor league baseball (4,6)
27. Paltrow (7)
29. Boxing, Million Dollar _____ (4)
31. John Woo, _____ Boiled (4)

#7

Across

5. "Hasta la vista, ____" (4)
7. Won best actress in 2002 for The Hours (6,6)
10. Juno is about an unplanned (9)
11. Will Hunting works as a ____ (7)
13. Minelli (4)
14. Highest grossing movie 2013, based on book (3,6,5)
16. Safdie brothers, Good ____ (4)
20. Tony Montana born in (4)
21. Director of Snatch (3,7)
23. E.T. the (5,11)
25. Nights of ____ (6)
27. Follow the yellow brick ____ (4)
29. Boxing, When We Were ____ (5)
31. Godzilla vs. ____ (4)
34. 1980, Richard Gere, Paul Schrader (8,6)
35. Sunset Boulevard character name (5,7)

Down

1. Star of Sideways, Paul ____ (8)
2. Almodovar (5)
3. ____ M for Muder (4)
4. Adam Driver and Scarlett Johansson get divorced (8,5)
6. What Ever Happened to ____ (4,4)
8. "Work sucks" (6,5)
9. The Wolf of ____ (4,6)
12. Six Degrees of ____ (10)
15. Director of The Deer Hunter (7,6)
17. "A ____. Shaken, not stirred." (7)
18. Genre of Die Hard (6)
19. Director, Stanley ____ (7)
22. Annie ____ (4)
24. Paper ____ (4)
26. To infinity and ____ (6)
27. Highest grossing movie of 1976 (5)
28. "As God is my witness, I'll never be hungry ____" (5)
30. Shallow ____ (5)
32. Paddington is a ____ (4)
33. A Star Is ____ (4)

#8

Across

1. 10 Things I Hate _____ (5,3)
3. Becomes a kingpin from the slums of Rio (4,2,3)
6. Man with scissors for hands (6)
8. The Kissing _____ (5)
10. Decision to _____ (5)
11. An American Werewolf in _____ (6)
12. Jim Carrey, Bruce _____ (8)
14. Stuck in a lamp for 10,000 years (5)
16. "Sometimes, dead is better" (3,8)
18. Animated, Finding _____ (4)
20. Boogie _____ (6)
21. Movie about fraudulent DC reporter Stephen Glass (9,5)
23. Taste of _____ (6)
25. Harry Potter actor, Daniel (9)
26. American Beauty director (3,6)
28. The Ides of _____, Clooney, Gosling (5)
29. Led Zeppelin concert film, The Song Remains the _____ (4)
30. Robert Pattinson Twilight character (6,6)
31. Rosebud is a reference to Kane's childhood _____ (4)

Down

1. Sang the theme song for Skyfall (5)
2. Quentin _____ (9)
3. "Keep your friends close, but your enemies _____" (6)
4. "Coffee is for closers" (9,4,4)
5. Twins 1988, short (6)
7. Animated movie about a trash collecting robot (5)
8. _____ and Clyde (6)
9. Michael Mann crime movie set in LA, Pacino, De Niro (4)
13. Director of Taxi Driver (6,8)
14. Won best actor in 1971 for The French Connection (4,7)
15. Deaf drummer, Sound of _____ (5)
16. Won best actress in 1963 for Hud (8,4)
17. Ben Affleck brother (5)
19. The _____ Diaries, vehicle (10)
22. Fictional land in Frozen (9)
24. Jason Schwartzman stars in this Wes Anderson movie about a high schooler (8)
27. Harold and _____ (5)

#9

Across

1. The Matrix director (9)
5. James Bond thriller (7)
9. Scenes From a _____ (8)
10. How to Train Your _____ (6)
13. "Mother of mercy, is this the end of _____" (4)
15. Paul Newman plays a lawyer with a _____ problem in The Verdict (8)
17. Sequel to The Shining (6,5)
19. What's Eating Gilbert _____ (5)
21. Altman LA, Short _____ (4)
22. Depp, The Ninth _____ (4)
24. Won best actress in 2012 for Silver Linings Playbook (8,8)
25. Shrek's accent (8)
28. All the President's Men is about this scandal (9)
31. Star of Body Heat, William _____ (4)
32. Giant ape in New York (4,4)
33. Raging Bull based on this boxer (4,7)
34. Reservoir _____ (4)

Down

1. Polanski, The Ghost _____ (6)
2. "If you build it, he will _____" (4)
3. Company that produces Batman (6,8)
4. Won best actress in 1944 for Gaslight (6,7)
6. Nicole _____ (6)
7. Wahlberg and Witherspoon teen movie (4)
8. LA LA _____ (4)
11. The Count of _____ (5,6)
12. "Forget it, _____, it's Chinatown" (4)
14. Tony Stark (4,3)
16. Judgment at _____ (9)
18. Lord of the Rings director (5,7)
20. The English _____ (7)
23. Double _____, femme fatale (9)
24. Woody Allen, Blue _____ (7)
26. Schindler (5)
27. Head of this animal, The Godfather (5)
29. Space movie, _____ 13 (6)
30. Silver Linings Playbook sports team (6)

#10

Across

1. Jack Nicholson, As Good _____ (2,2,4)
5. Doug in The Hangover is found on the _____ (4)
6. Planet of the _____ (4)
10. Person who rates films (6)
11. 2001, A Beautiful _____ (4)
12. Nicolas Cage, Raising _____ (7)
14. Photographer who operated movie camera (9)
16. Colin Farrell follows orders from a phone (5,5)
18. Coppola, not Francis (5)
20. Star of The Player (3,7)
21. CIA agent who helps James Bond (5,6)
22. Fever Pitch, Jimmy Fallon is a fan of this team (3,3)
24. Won best actor in 1947 A Double Life (6,6)
25. Dan In Real _____ (4)
26. Buy this for a seat (6)
28. Won best actress in 1969 for The Prime of Miss Jean Brodie (6,5)
31. Billy Bob Thornton Christmas movie (3,5)
32. Can calm the Hulk down (7)
33. Scientist in Back to the Future (3,5)
34. Director of westerns, Sergio _____ (5)
35. Ridley Scott's brother (4)

Down

2. Won best actress in 2011 for portayal of Margaret Thatcher (6)
3. Dorothy and _____ (4)
4. College baseball team, Everybody Wants _____!! (4)
5. The _____, worn on finger (4)
7. Licorice _____ (5)
8. Won best actor in 1955 for Marty (6,8)
9. Won best actor in 1929 In Old Arizona (6,6)
13. _____ of the Body Snatchers (8)
14. Won best actor in 1933 The Private Life of Henry VIII (7,8)
15. State The Help takes place in (11)
17. Won best actress in 2018 for The Favourite (6,6)
19. Won best actor in 1946 The Best Years of Our Lives (7,5)
23. Horror director, Ti _____ (4)
27. Bad guy in Avengers End Game (6)
29. "I am big! It's the pictures that got _____" (5)
30. The Grand Budapest _____ (5)

#11

Across

2. Won best actress in 1938 for Jezebel (5,5)
5. Won best actor in 1938 Boys Town, Spencer _____ (5)
6. My Neighbor _____ (6)
7. Peter O'_____ (5)
9. Lancaster (4)
12. Bogart's character in The African Queen (7,6)
14. Guardians of the _____ (6)
15. Western, True _____ (4)
16. A Time to _____, Grisham (4)
18. Highest grossing movie 2020, Will Smith (3,4,3,4)
22. Vince Vaughn and Owen Wilson 2005 (7,8)
23. Princess in Shrek (5)
24. Wrote the Halloween theme music (4,9)
25. Steve McQueen disaster movie, The Towering _____ (7)
28. Jim Carrey born in (6)
29. "I'm as mad as hell, and I'm not going to take this _____!" (7)
30. Jerry Maguire's job (6,5)

Down

1. Dog in Wizard of Oz (4)
2. Django's wife (10)
3. Will Smith character in Independence Day (6,6)
4. Who's Afraid of Roger _____ (6)
8. Indian Hollywood (9)
10. A curse is placed on a loan officer, Drag Me _____ (2,4)
11. Director of Clerks (5,5)
13. Maggie Gyllenhaal's brother (4)
15. Won best actor in 1970 for Patton (6,1,5)
17. Won best actress in 1936 for The Great Ziegfeld (5,6)
19. Paul Newman pool player (4,5)
20. Unknown creature invades spacecraft (5)
21. The Last House on the _____ (4)
22. "Gentlemen, you can't fight in here! This is the _____" (3,4)
24. Tommy Lee _____ (5)
25. My Own Private _____ (5)
26. The People vs. Larry _____ (5)
27. Stars at _____ (4)

#12

Across

2 "Is it ____?" (4)
6 Letters from Iwo ____ (4)
7 Alan Rickman first role in film (3,4)
11 2017, Lady ____ (4)
12 Won best actor in 1931 A Free Soul (6,9)
14 Vietnam vet gets revenge 1977 (7,7)
16 All That ____, Fosse (4)
17 Ethan Hawke plays a serial killer, 2022 (5,5)
22 The Good, the Bad and the ____ (4)
23 Who's Afraid of ____ (8,5)
26 Scottish warrior leads rebellion against England (10)
27 Memento director (11,5)
30 3:10 to ____ (4)
31 Number of times A Star is Born has been made (4)
32 Being John ____ (9)
33 The Big ____, Noir (5)
34 Cronenberg car movie, James Spader (5)

Down

1 Super 8 director (2,6)
2 Happy Gilmore (7)
3 ____ Streep (5)
4 Plays Sally in When Harry Met Sally (3,4)
5 Jack Skellington is king of ____ (9,4)
8 Cheaper by the ____ (5)
9 24 Hour Party ____ (6)
10 Harrison Ford looks for missing wife in Paris (7)
13 Trainspotting city (9)
15 Won best actress in 2001 for Monster's Ball (5,5)
18 Finding Nemo won the oscar for Best ____ Feature (8)
19 Annie in Bridesmaids (7,4)
20 A Clockwork Orange director (7)
21 Scorsese comedy starring Griffin Dunne (5,5)
24 Young drummer and his instructor (8)
25 Highest grossing movie of 1975 (4)
28 Lady and the ____ (5)
29 Directed Us, Jordan ____ (5)

#13

Across

7. Voices of the dead are heard through this horror film's static (11)
8. A quest for the Holy Grail, not always serious but always hilarious (5,6)
9. The silent film star known as 'The Tramp.' (7)
10. The Hogwarts house known for bravery (10)
14. Quentin Tarantino's bloody bride (7,5)
16. No Country for _____ (3,3)
17. This ship couldn't dodge an iceberg in its 1997 blockbuster (7)
19. The color of the pill Neo took to leave the Matrix (3)
21. The Edge of _____ (9)
23. The fictional African country where Black Panther reigns (7)
25. Director of Pulp Fiction (9)
26. The Grapes of _____ (5)
27. Pixar movie where emotions run wild inside a young girl's mind (6,3)
28. A dreamy city of stars, love, and jazz (2,2,4)

Down

1. A dream within a dream within a dream, directed by Christopher Nolan (9)
2. Won best acress in 1968 for Funny Girl (9)
3. This 'beautiful' mind belonged to a Nobel laureate (4,4)
4. She journeys from Kansas to Oz (7)
5. He 'made an offer' nobody could refuse in 'The Godfather.' (4,8)
6. The 'Greatest Showman' who brought the circus to life (1,1,6)
11. This movie features a shark named Bruce (7,4)
12. Schindler's _____ (4)
13. This superhero's weakness is a green mineral (8)
14. Uma Thurman, Kill _____ (4)
15. Dog in The Sandlot (3,5)
18. The galaxy's most famous Wookiee (9)
19. The Italian Stallion in the boxing ring (5)
20. A board game that comes to life, starring Robin Williams (7)
22. First name of the archaeologist who hates snakes (7)
24. 'Why so serious?' asks this villain (5)

#14

Across

2. Love & _____ (10)
6. Shadow of a _____ (5)
9. Kurt _____ (7)
11. Titanic unsinkable Molly _____ (5)
13. Shaun of the _____ (4)
14. Driving Miss _____ (5)
15. Based on a Stephen King book, The Dead _____ (4)
16. Highest grossing movie of 1985, time travel (4,2,3,6)
17. Uncut _____ (4)
19. Tarantino book 2022 (6,11)
24. Boston Globe movie (9)
25. The Place Beyond the _____ (5)
26. Scarface main character (4,7)
30. Highest grossing movie of 1977 (4,4)
32. Under the Silver _____ (4)
33. Highest grossing movie of 1972 (3,9)
34. Person who shows you to your seat (5)

Down

1. Benedict _____ (11)
3. Sounds added to the film (5,7)
4. Plays Harry in When Harry Met Sally (5,7)
5. "There's no place _____" (4,4)
7. Denzel Washington football movie, Remember _____ (3,6)
8. Hacksaw _____ (5)
10. The Boondock _____ (6)
12. Johnny Cash movie (4,3,4)
17. Won best actor in 1930 Disraeli (6,6)
18. Rocky Horror Picture _____ (4)
20. Brad Pitt in space (2,5)
21. Won best actor in 1986 for The Color of Money (4,6)
22. Jessica in American Pie, Natasha _____ (6)
23. Pan's Labyrinth language (7)
27. Beverly Hills Cop (6)
28. One who acts (5)
29. Saturday Night _____ (5)
31. O Brother, Where Art _____ (4)

#15

Across

2. Job of main characters in Pulp Fiction (6)
5. Star of Die Hard (5,6)
9. 1948, Bicycle _____ (7)
10. Fargo setting (9)
12. "Yo, Adrian!" (5)
14. First public performance (8)
16. Won best actor in 1961 for Judgment at Nuremberg (10,6)
17. Star of Barton Fink, John _____ (8)
19. Won best actor in 1999 for American Beauty (5,6)
20. Mildred _____ (6)
24. Scarface city (5)
27. _____ Zellweger (5)
29. Spielberg movie about his childhood (3,9)
30. Christmas movie, Love _____ (8)
31. Starship _____ (8)
32. Hurrican coming towards a hotel of mobsters, 1948 (3,5)

Down

1. Walter Hill, biker friends, Streets of _____ (4)
3. Puritan police man searches for missing girl on a Scottish village (3,6,3)
4. The _____ Gun, comedy (5)
5. Played Mrs.Robinson in The Graduate (8)
6. Sandler remote control (5)
7. Song that opened Saturday Night Fever (6,5)
8. Won best actress in 2004 for Million Dollar Baby (6,5)
11. Hotel in The Shining (8)
13. "What we've got here is failure to _____" (11)
14. Jackie Brown star (3,5)
15. Car in Back to the Future (8)
18. "I'll be back" (10)
21. Mr._____ Goes to Washington (5)
22. Indiana Jones and the Last _____ (7)
23. Ace _____ (7)
25. David Lynch, Kyle MacLachlan, Blue _____ (6)
26. The Fault In Our _____ (5)
28. Fish with short-term memory loss (4)

#16

Across

2. Won best actor in 1962 for To Kill a Mockingbird (7,4)
7. Killer shark (4)
10. Sing _____ (6)
11. Dirk Diggler (6,6)
13. The Spy Who _____ Me (7)
14. Director of Nashville and Short Cuts (6,6)
16. Highest grossing movie of 1978, musical (6)
17. Man on Fire star (6,10)
22. Won best actor in 1939 Goodbye, Mr. Chips (6,5)
25. Fox and His _____ (7)
26. Plays Madea in the Madea movies (5,5)
27. Vince Vaughn, Jon Favreau, wannabe actors and dating life (8)
28. Hoffman, Straw _____ (4)
29. Paul Newman and Robert Redford pull off a con (3,5)
30. Website The Social Network (8)
32. Won best actor for his portrayal of Churchill in 2017 (4,6)
33. Marlon _____ (6)

Down

1. Good Will Hunting city (6)
2. Won best actor in 1952 for High Noon (4,6)
3. Peggy Sue _____ (3,7)
4. _____ Without a Cause (5)
5. The Blair Witch _____ (7)
6. Director and star of Unforgiven (5,8)
7. Park owner in Jurassic Park (4,7)
8. Won Oscar for best actor, King Richard (4,5)
9. Ryan in Saving Private Ryan (4,5)
12. Western made in Italy (9)
15. Highest grossing movie 2019 (8,7)
16. Paths of ____ (5)
18. James Cameron guest starred in this HBO series (9)
19. Captain Jack (7)
20. Witness for the _____ (11)
21. 12 Angry Men is about a (4)
23. Kidman, wants to be a famous reporter (2,3,3)
24. Bee Movie (8)
29. "Toga! _____" (4)
30. Eastwood secret service agent, In The Line of _____ (4)
31. The Lion _____ (4)

#17

Across

3. Adam Sandler plays a basketball scout, 2022 (6)
7. Cars, Lightning _____ (7)
9. Lars Von Trier, Kidman, on stage (8)
11. Jamie Foxx as freed slave (6)
13. All the President's Men paper (10,4)
15. In the Name of the _____ (6)
17. "Here's ____" Nicholson (6)
19. The Maltese _____ (6)
21. Forrest _____ (4)
23. Charlie is looking for the _____ _____ (6,6)
24. State Foxcatcher takes place in (12)
26. Sissy _____ (6)
27. Mighty Ducks sport (6)
29. Rob Reiner comedy about an England band (4,2,6,3)
32. The Cotton _____ (4)
33. Crouching Tiger, ____ (6,6)
34. Team of superheroes (8)
35. Highest grossing movie of 1988, Tom Cruise (4,3)

Down

1. Actor that plays the Joker in Dark Knight (6)
2. Villain in Saw (6)
4. Mel Gibson aliens (5)
5. Orlando Bloom Lord Of The Rings character (7)
6. The Dark Knight _____ (5)
7. Short term memory loss, finding wife's murderer (7)
8. True Romance writer, _____ Tarantino (7)
10. Won best actor in 1981 for On Golden Pond (5,5)
12. Won best actress in 2021 for The Eyes of Tammy Faye (7,8)
14. V for ____ (8)
16. _____ Together, Kar-Wai Won (5)
18. Margot Robbie DC character (6,5)
20. Won best actress in 1950 for Born Yesterday (4,8)
22. Stephen Hawking, The Theory of _____ (10)
23. Plays Willy Wonka (4,6)
25. "Soylent Green is _____" (6)
28. The Lord of the _____ (5)
30. Highest grossing movie of 2004, animated sequel (5,1)
31. Liam Neeson is looking for his daughter (5)

#18

Across

1. Gus Van ___ (4)
6. Person who moves the camera (4)
7. The Godfather (6,6)
8. ___ v Ferrari (4)
10. Won best actress in 1985 for The Trip to Bountiful (9,4)
12. Our Idiot ___ (7)
15. Won best actor for Capote (6,7,7)
17. The Red ___ (5)
18. The Hand that Rocks the ___ (6)
20. People watching the movie (8)
22. Sang the theme song for You Only Live Twice (5,7)
24. "Frankly, my dear, I don't give a ___" (4)
25. Life of Pi director (3,3)
26. Star of Platoon (5)
27. William Hurt, crime noir in FL (4,4)
28. ___ Strawberries (4)
29. Richard Gere and Julia Roberts (6,5)
30. Mads, star of The Hunt (9)
31. Matt Damon goes to Mars (3,7)
32. End of ___ (5)

Down

1. The Virgin Suicides director (5,7)
2. Won best actor in 1944 Going My Way" (4,6)
3. Won best actress in 1992 for Howards End (4,8)
4. Director of The Breakfast Club (4,6)
5. Marlin's wife in Finding Nemo (5)
9. Rated R (10)
11. 1994 crime movie, star studded cast (4,7)
13. Won best actress in 1934 for It Happened One Night (9,7)
14. Mary Jane in early 2000s Spiderman movies (7,5)
16. Paris, (5)
19. Lethal Weapon star (3,6)
21. Kill Bill (3,7)
23. The French ___ (10)
25. Tim Burton, Mars ___! (7)

#19

Across

2. Plays Captain America (5,5)
5. "Say 'hello' to my little _____" (6)
8. Highest grossing movie of 1973, Horror (3,9)
10. Sunrise at _____ (10)
11. World where no kids are born anymore, Children _____ (2,3)
13. Howl's Moving _____ (6)
14. Starred in two movies about JFK (5,7)
16. Being John Malkovich director (5,5)
18. Kung Fu _____, animated (5)
20. Won best actress in 1983 for Terms of Endearment (7,8)
22. Rebel Without a _____ (5)
25. Highest grossing movie of 1970, Ali MacGraw (4,5)
27. Won best actress in 1931 for Min and Bill (5,8)
28. Hotel in Ocean's Eleven, The _____ (8)
29. Taxi _____ (6)
30. Michael, The Godfather (6)
31. Portrait of a Lady _____ (2,4)
32. Won best actress in 1973 for A Touch of Class (6,7)
33. Civil War movie, Denzel, Broderick (5)
34. Blades of Glory sport (3,7)

Down

1. Channing Tatum stripper movie (5,4)
2. One Flew Over the _____ (7,4)
3. Man of _____ (5)
4. Penn, Walken, rural PA (2,5,5)
5. "Louis, I think this is the beginning of a beautiful _____" (10)
6. ""You ain't heard _____ yet!" (6)
7. Won best actor in 1965 for Cat Ballou (3,6)
8. Kids discover a map and look for treasure (3,7)
9. Voices Buzz in Toy Story (3,5)
12. Director of Bowling for Columbine (7,5)
15. Won best actress in 1937 for The Good Earth, Luise _____ (6)
17. Highest grossing movie of 1993 (8,4)
19. Tom Hanks, Cloud _____ (5)
21. Ed Norton is going to jail in the morning, 25th _____ (4)
23. The _____ Spider-Man (7)
24. Director of Inside Man (5,3)
25. "The Dude" (8)
26. Laurence _____ (7)
29. Isle of _____ (4)
30. A Quiet _____ (5)

#20

Across

1. Jim Carrey's costar in Dumb and Dumber (4,7)
4. Horror, Mid_____ (6)
7. Won best actress in 2008 for The Reader (4,7)
8. Dallas Buyers _____ (4)
11. The Thing takes place in _____ (10)
13. The Untouchables city (7)
16. Plays Lisa in Rear Window, Grace _____ (5)
17. Won best actress in 1964 for Mary Poppins (5,7)
18. Let the Right _____ (3,2)
19. Director of JFK (6,5)
21. Man on _____ (4)
22. Heat is set in _____ (3,7)
26. Won best actor in 1954 for On the Waterfront (6)
27. Fletch was remade in 2022 with this actor (3,4)
28. Highest grossing movie of 1987 (5,3,3,1,4)
29. The Fisher _____ (4)
31. One False _____ (4)
32. A written form of musical composition (5)
33. ____ Phoenix, brother is also an actor (5)
34. Casino city (3,5)
35. Falls from the sky at the end of Magnolia (5)

Down

2. Back to the _____ (6)
3. Plays main character in Clueless (6,11)
5. Winding road in Los Angeles (10)
6. Won best actress in 1972 for Cabaret (4,8)
7. Won best actress in 1981 for On Golden Pond (9,7)
9. Name of Police Chief in Jaws (5)
10. Director of Red River, Howard _____ (5)
12. The Thomas Crown _____ (6)
13. Shown at end of movie (7)
14. Tom Hanks plays a pilot (5)
15. Won best actress in 1943 for The Song of Bernadette (8,5)
20. _____ of a Murder (7)
21. The _____ Element (5)
22. Yorgos ____ (9)
23. Frank Sinatra won an Oscar for this movie, From Here To _____ (8)
24. Diary of a _____ (5,3)
25. Tom Hanks in the suburbs (3,5)
30. Boogie Nights, Roller _____ (4)

#21

Across

2. Won best actress in 1976 for Network (4,7)
7. Star of Barry Lyndon, Ryan ____ (5)
8. It's a Wonderful Life holiday (9)
12. Won best actress in 1952 for Come Back, Little Sheba (7,5)
13. Edward Norton, 1998, American _____ _ (7,1)
16. Crimes of the _____ (6)
18. Won best actress in 1991 for The Silence of the Lambs (5,6)
19. Zombie_____ (4)
20. A Hard Day's _____ (5)
21. Gosling and Crowe, The _____ (4,4)
25. Played the little girl in E.T. (4,9)
26. Won best actor in 1968 for Charly (5,9)
27. Steve Martin, Father of the _____ (5)
28. Won best actor in 1935 The Informer (6,8)
30. Donald _____ (6)
32. Silence of the _____ (5)
33. Highest grossing rated R movie (5)
34. Marriage _____ (5)
35. Lady Bird (7,5)
36. Tonya Harding movie (1,5)

Down

1. _____ and Her Sisters (6)
3. Revenge of the _____ (5)
4. Denzel ____ (10)
5. The Mask of _____ (5)
6. Jodie ____ (6)
9. 1920s gangsters, Joel Coen (7,8)
10. Wolf of Wall Street based on life of this man (6,7)
11. Totoro (2,8)
14. Wendy in The Shining (7,6)
15. My Left _____ (4)
17. Actor who plays Spiderman in 2002 movie (4,7)
22. 2018 best picture winner (5,4)
23. Won best actress in 1942 for Mrs. Miniver (5,6)
24. A line (5)
29. Sophie's _____ (6)
31. Small-time boxer becomes champion (5)

#22

Across

1. Actor who plays Gordan Gekko's protégé (7,5)
5. _____ Fink (6)
6. White Men Can't _____ (4)
7. Who Framed Roger _____ ? (6)
11. Directed Gravity, Alfonso _____ (6)
13. Woman in Navy SEALS training (2,4)
15. Midnight in _____ (5)
17. Won best actor in 1937 Captain Courageous (7,5)
18. Star of The Bourne Identity (5)
19. Won best actress in 2003 for Monster (8,6)
21. Shanghai _____ (7)
23. Star of The 40 Year Old Virgin (7)
24. "Show me the _____!!!!" (5)
25. Director of The Producers (3,6)
27. Suddenly, Last _____ (6)
29. Star of American Sniper (7,6)
31. Highest grossing movie 2012 (3,8)
33. 2007 George Clooney movie (7,7)
34. Rounders is about (5)
35. Paul Thomas _____ (8)

Down

2. Won best actress in 1966 for Who's Afraid of Virginia Woolf (9,6)
3. Robin _____ (4)
4. Won best actor in 1984 for Amadeus (1,6,7)
5. Mickey Rourke plays a drunk (6)
8. Scarface director (5,2,5)
9. Won best actress in 2014 for Still Alice (8,5)
10. Won best actor in 2000 for Gladiator (7,5)
12. The King's _____ (6)
14. _____ and Alexander (5)
16. Old astronauts (5,7)
20. Won best actor in 1983 for Tender Mercies (6,6)
22. Kristen Stewart, Princess Diana (7)
26. Dead Poets _____ (7)
27. Meryl _____ (6)
28. Anne Hathaway, Rachel Getting _____ (7)
30. Lena Dunham, Sharp _____ (5)
32. Director, Christopher _____ (5)

#23

Across

2. Scenes that are filmed but not used (8)
6. Donnie Brasco star (6)
10. Al Pacino, cuban drug dealer (8)
12. "I'm going to make him an offer he can't _____" (6)
13. Edward _____, Burton, Depp (12)
14. I, _____ Blake (6)
16. Won best actor in 1960 for Elmer Gantry (4,9)
18. Won best actress in 1949 for The Heiress (6,2,9)
23. Won best actress in 2010 for Black Swan (7,7)
26. Something you can't refuse (2,5)
27. Won best actress in 1977 for Annie Hall (5,6)
30. "E.T. phone _____" (4)
31. In the _____, Todd Field (7)
32. Iron Man (4,5)
33. Ford v _____ (7)
34. Pitt and Freeman cop movie (5)
35. "We're not in _____ anymore" (6)
36. Psycho has a famous scene in a (6)
37. Breakfast at _____ (8)

Down

1. "Listen to them. Children of the night. What ____ they make." (5)
3. Lost in _____ (11)
4. Won best actor in 1940 The Philadelphia Story, James ____ (7)
5. Thor: Love and _____ (7)
7. "Forget it, Jake, it's _____" (9)
8. The Chronicles of _____, based on book series (6)
9. Once Upon a Time in _____ (9)
11. Heath Ledger born in (9)
15. Gemini Man, ____ Smith (4)
17. Fanny & _____ (9)
19. Full Metal Jacket (7)
20. Won best actor in 1974 for Harry and Tonto (3,6)
21. The Girl with the _____ (6,6)
22. Tom Cruise is Jack _____ (7)
24. Won best actor for The Pianist in 2002 (6,5)
25. Sopranos movie, The Many Saints ____ (2,6)
28. Star of Birdman (6)
29. Two hit men in Belgium, Colin Farrell (2,6)
32. No Country for Old Men state (5)

#24

Across

1. Stand by Me based on book by Stephen ____ (4)
4. Rocky (8)
6. Tom Hanks stranded (4,4)
9. Sidney ____ (7)
12. In Girls Trip they travel to this city (3,7)
13. Den of ____ (7)
14. 1997 Noir, based on James Ellroy novel (2,12)
17. The Blues ____ (8)
20. "They call me Mister ____" (5)
24. Plays Mr. Pink in Reservoir Dogs (5,7)
26. Nonfiction film (11)
28. Star of original Pink Panther movies (5,7)
29. Thief who enters people's dreams (9)
30. DiCaprio, Shutter ____ (6)
33. Won best actor in 1932 Dr. Jekyll and Mr. Hyde (7,5)
34. "If you've got a taste for terror… take ____ to the prom" (6)
35. Won best actor in 1928 The Last Command The Way of All Flesh (4,8)

Down

2. As Good as ____ (2,4)
3. Seven who fought like 700 (11,5)
4. Wrote Scarface (5)
5. Won best actress in 2016 for La La Land (4,5)
7. Lucky Number ____ (6)
8. Anthony Perkins in Psycho (6,5)
10. Small town horror, 1958, remade in 1988 (3,4)
11. Plays the mentor in Good Will Hunting (5,8)
15. Highest grossing movie 1997 (7)
16. Sonny Corleone actor (5,4)
18. Rebel Without a Cause landmark, Griffith ____ (11)
19. "I feel the need—the need for ____" (5)
21. "I have always depended on the kindness of ____" (9)
22. Fast and Furious franchise is about (6)
23. Story of growing up filmed over 12 years (7)
25. Casablanca setting (8)
27. G (7)
28. Favorite movie theater snack (7)
31. Crazy, Stupid, ____ (4)
32. "Fasten your seatbelts. It's going to be a bumpy ____" (5)

#25

Across

2. Road to _____ (9)
4. Won best actor in 1975 for One Flew Over the Cuckoo's Nest (9)
9. Chris Pratt character in Jurassic World (4,5)
11. Forrest Gump home state (7)
13. The _____ Job, heist (7)
14. Amy Adams communicates with aliens (7)
16. Braveheart, Robert the _____ (5)
17. Won best actress in 2013 for Blue Jasmine (4,9)
19. Star of Fight Club, not Brad Pitt (6,6)
21. Clint Eastwood cop movie (5,5)
22. Number of white stripes Nemo has (5)
23. Voice of Marlin in Finding Nemo (6,6)
26. Tom Cruise, Minority _____ (6)
27. The Social ____ (7)
28. Won best actor in 1972 for The Godfather (6,6)
31. The Green Mile takes place in a ____ (6)
33. Won best actress in 1951 for A Streetcar Named Desire (6,5)
34. Won best actor in 1942 Yankee Doodle Dandy (5,6)
35. Hunger Games main character (7)

Down

1. Won best actress in 1955 for The Rose Tattoo (4,7)
3. "Attica! Attica!" (3,3,9)
5. Kathy Bates, Dolores _____ (9)
6. Enemy of the _____ (5)
7. Amadeus is about the life of (6)
8. The Red Shoes is about a _____ dancer (6)
10. The ____ Queen, John Huston, Bogart, Hepburn (7)
12. Star of Batman (1989) (7,6)
15. Platoon is about this war (7)
17. Jodie Foster's character in The Silence of the Lambs (7,8)
18. The Coen _____ (8)
20. Close Encounters of the _____ (5,4)
22. Singin' in _____ (3,4)
24. Knocked Up star (4,5)
25. The Cabin in the _____ (5)
29. A Streetcar Named _____ (6)
30. Rami ____ (5)
32. Shakespeare in ____ (4)

#26

Across

6. Lock, Stock and Two Smoking ____ (7)
8. Actress who plays Lara in Doctor Zhivago (5,8)
9. Peter Jackson directed a documentary about this band (3,7)
11. Dirty Harry _____ (8)
13. Star of Juno (6,4)
18. The Hudsucker _____ (5)
19. Animated, rhymes with utopia (8)
20. Highest grossing movie of 1998 (6,7,4)
23. "I'll have what she's _____" (6)
24. Rob Lowe and James Spader friendship, 1990 (3,9)
27. Moonrise _____ (7)
28. 1986 David Lynch movie (4,6)
30. Won best actor in 1977 for The Goodbye Girl (7,8)
31. Bonnie and _____ (5)
32. Oliver Stone Vietnam movie 1986 (7)
33. 1953, parents visit children in Tokyo (5,5)

Down

1. Won best actor in 1992 for Scent of a Woman (2,6)
2. Harry Potter, Ron _____ (7)
3. Rocky set in this city (12)
4. Won best actor in 1987 for Wall Street (7,7)
5. Nicole Kidman's husband is reincarnated as a 10 year old boy (5)
6. The story of a young deer (5)
7. Punch Drunk ____ (4)
8. Won best actress in 1970 for Women in Love, Glenda _____ (7)
10. _____ Smell of Success (5)
12. Monty Python and the _____ (4,5)
14. "Who you gonna call?" (12)
15. Won best actress in 1960 for Butterfield 8 (9,6)
16. Highest grossing movie of 2008 (3,4,6)
17. Denzel and Ethan Hawke cop movie (8,3)
21. Born on the Fourth of July is based on (3,5)
22. Sandler, Hubie _____ (9)
25. Type of dissolve edit (4,3)
26. Legally _____ (6)
29. Howard Hanks, John Wayne, Rio ____ (5)

#27

Across

- **3** Breaking the ____ (5)
- **7** Tom Hanks job in Philadelphia (6)
- **12** Won best actress in 1961 for Two Women (6,5)
- **13** Star of Rosemary's Baby (3,6)
- **14** Alien superhero who grows up on Earth (8)
- **15** Won best actress in 2000 for Erin Brockovich (5,7)
- **18** The Color ____ (6)
- **19** Star of The Batman, 2022 (9)
- **22** Won best actor in 1959 for Ben-Hur (8,6)
- **24** Almost Famous director, Cameron (5)
- **25** The Wild ____, western (5)
- **26** Lord of the Rings based on novels by J.R.R. ____ (7)
- **29** "I see dead people" (5,5)
- **31** 2022 horror movie, people smiling (5)
- **32** Söze (6)
- **33** Denzel Washington portrayed this civil rights leader (7,1)
- **34** Won best actress in 1948 for Johnny Belinda (4,5)
- **35** Ship in Alien (8)

Down

- **1** Wear these to watch a 3-D movie (7)
- **2** Monty ____ (6)
- **4** Won best actor in 1963 for Lilies of the Field (6,7)
- **5** Ryan Gosling is a drug addicted teacher (4,6)
- **6** Scream original title (5,5)
- **8** Patrick Swayze bouncer (4,5)
- **9** Rebel Without a Cause actor (5,4)
- **10** Joaquin ____ (7)
- **11** Won best actor for Joker (7,7)
- **16** ____ and the Sundance Kid (5,7)
- **17** From Russia with ____ (4)
- **20** Eternal Sunshine of the ____ (8,4)
- **21** Oscar nom for Lord of the Rings, Ian ____ (8)
- **23** Freed the Genie (7)
- **26** Ben Affleck robbery in Boston (3,4)
- **27** JFK is about District Attorney Jim ____ (8)
- **28** Sharon Stone and Robert De Niro are married, Scorsese (6)
- **29** Number of Connery James Bond movies (5)
- **30** Spencer ____ (5)

#28

Across

1 The _____ Dozen (5)
4 The Piano _____ (7)
7 A Fistful of _____ (7)
11 Highest grossing movie of 1996, 7/4 (12,3)
12 James Caan heist movie (5)
13 Ant Man actor (4,4)
15 Shot from above (6)
17 Indiana Jones (8,4)
19 Harry Potter spin off franchise (9,6)
22 Won best actress in 1979 for Norma Rae, Sally _____ (5)
25 Won Oscar for best actress three times (9)
27 Highest grossing movie of all time (6)
28 The Sandlot sport (8)
30 The 40 Year Old _____ (6)
31 Trapped at sea with a tiger (4,2,2)
32 RoboCop city (7)
33 Alien, Ellen _____ (6)
34 Star of Zombieland, Jesse _____ (9)
35 Won best actress in 1988 for The Accused (6)

Down

1 Won best actor in 1979 for Kramer vs. Kramer (6,7)
2 Scent of a _____ (5)
3 First Daniel Craig James Bond (6,6)
5 Sandler golf movie (5,7)
6 Won best actor in 1945 The Lost Weekend (3,7)
8 Snow White and the _____ (5,6)
9 Alien director (6,5)
10 Clint Eastwood movie released in 2021 (3,5)
14 Coach in Any Given Sunday (2,6)
16 Won best actress in 1989 for Driving Miss Daisy (7,5)
18 Code in Matrix comes from these (5,7)
20 Baby deer (5)
21 Plays the ingénue in All About Eve (4,6)
23 Mulholland _____ (5)
24 Diamonds Are _____ (7)
26 Embarrassing mistake (7)
29 Mrs. Harris Goes to _____ (5)

#29

Across

1. The strong silent type, Gary _____ (6)
3. True Romance director (4,5)
7. ____, Texas (5)
8. Insomnia set in (6)
10. Memories of _____ (6)
12. Howard Ratner, Uncut Gems (4,7)
14. Movies that are coming soon (7)
17. Walk the Line is about the life of this musician (6,4)
19. Wings of _____ (6)
22. Won best actor in 1953 for Stalag 17 (7,6)
23. "Elementary, my dear ____" (6)
24. The Rock, Jungle _____ (6)
25. Moneyball based on real life of (5,5)
27. Director of The Princess Bride (3,6)
29. There Will _____ (2,5)
31. Won best actor for Dallas Buyers Club (11)
32. Sixteen Candles, _____ Ringwald (5)
33. NBA star who appears in Uncut Gems (5,7)
34. "We rob _____" (5)

Down

2. Dennis Hopper and Peter Fonda, road trip (4,5)
3. Strangers on a _____ (5)
4. Voices Woody in Toy Story (3,5)
5. Mad Max: _____ (4,4)
6. The Cable Guy (6)
9. Directed Titanic (5,7)
11. Guillermo _____ (3,4)
13. Lethal Weapon stars Mel Gibson and (5,6)
15. Won best actress in 2005 for Walk the Line (5,11)
16. Bruce Willis character in Die Hard (4,7)
18. Won best actor in 1951 for The African Queen (8,6)
19. Faye _____ (7)
20. Won best actress in in 1974 for Alice Doesn't Live Here Anymore (5,7)
21. Foster Kane's last words (7)
26. Wakanda _____ (7)
28. Rachel, ____ (6)
30. The Simpsons _____ (5)

#30

Across

1. The Right _____, astronauts (5)
3. Star of Blue Velvet, Kyle _____ (10)
8. Won best actor in 1995 for Leaving Las Vegas (7,4)
9. Won best actress in 1928 for 7th Heaven (5,6)
10. Voice of Shrek (4,5)
12. Sarandon (5)
13. Indiana Jones day job (9)
15. Alice Doesn't Live _____ (4,7)
17. Titanic director (5,7)
20. Original James Bond (4,7)
21. A place to see a new movie (7)
22. Director, Oliver _____ (5)
25. Michael Mann serial killer movie (9)
26. Mouse in The Green Mile (2,7)
27. Kill Bill director (7,9)
28. _____ and Maude (6)
29. Taxi Driver (6,2,4)
30. Group of investors bet against the US mortgage market (3,3,5)
31. Julie Andrews is Mary _____ (7)
32. Keanu Reeves goes undercover as a surfer (5,5)

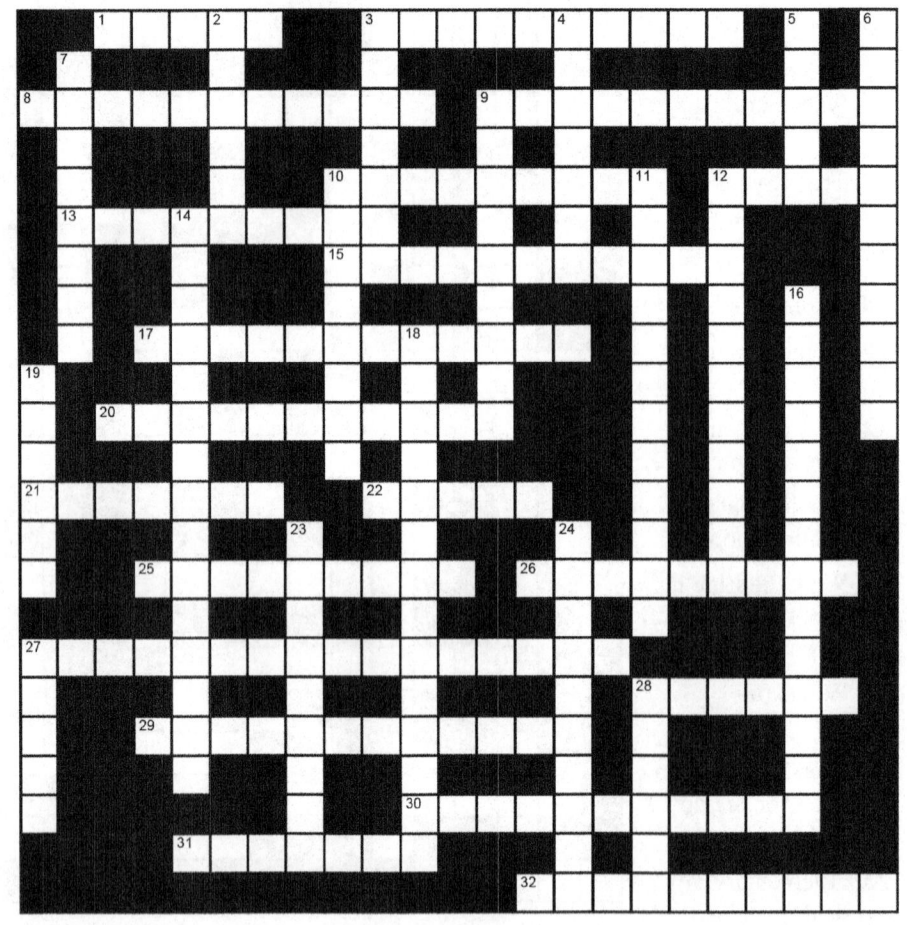

Down

2. Inglourious Basterds is set in this country (6)
3. Tom Cruise, Jerry _____ (7)
4. Plays Indiana Jones' dad (7)
5. Plays Forrest Gump (5)
6. Dr. _____ (11)
7. Leonardo _____ (8)
9. Plays the Grinch (2000) (3,6)
10. The Last of the _____ (8)
11. _____ vs. the World (5,7)
12. Misery is based on the book by (7,4)
14. Glenn Close and Michael Douglas thriller (5,10)
16. Spielberg won his best director Oscar for this (10,4)
18. "I have nipples Greg, could you milk me?" (4,3,7)
19. The Verdict takes place in this city (6)
23. Princess Bride (9)
24. Eastwood, car, neighbour (4,6)
27. Scratches the chalkboard in Jaws (5)
28. Dear Evan _____, based on broadway musical (6)

Across

1. Costner becomes friends with the boy he kidnapped, A Perfect ____ (5)
4. Sonic the _____ (8)
7. Won best actress in 1994 for Blue Sky (7,5)
9. Brothers who directed Dumb and Dumber (8)
10. "I am serious … and don't call me _____" (7)
11. My Best Friend's _____ (7)
14. Chris Washington's job in Get Out (12)
16. Basin City (3,4)
17. 2008 hit musical (4,3)
18. They Shoot Horses, _____ (4,4)
22. The Bridge on the _____ (5,4)
23. Director of Pink Flamingos and Hairspray (4,6)
27. Peggy Sue Got Married actress (8,6)
30. Won best actress in 2017 for Three Billboards (7,9)
31. Promising Young _____ (5)
32. Straight Outta _____ (7)
34. Shot tight on actor's face (5-2)
35. College comedy, Animal _____ (5)
36. Danny Boyle, Ewan McGregor drug movie (13)
37. Two NYC detectives, 1970s, The _____ Connection (6)

Down

2. Gosling car movie (5)
3. Plays washed up movie star in Lost in Translation (4,6)
4. Dazed and Confused is set here (4,6)
5. Michael Cimino 1980 box office bomb (7,4)
6. Sang the song "Call Me" American Gigolo soundtrack (7)
8. The Termintator is sent to kill (5,6)
10. Star of Hancock (5)
12. Christopher Nolan war movie (7)
13. Highest grossing movie of 1979, divorce (6,2,6)
15. Marlon Brando "could have been a contender" (2,3,10)
19. Played the president in The American President (7,7)
20. Slang for movie (5)
21. Won best actress in 1953 for Roman Holiday (7)
24. Won best actor for Milk in 2008 (4,4)
25. Johnny Knoxville (7)
26. A puppet becomes a real boy (9)
28. Director Pedro ____ (9)
29. _____ Arizona, Cage (7)
33. To Catch a _____ (5)

#32

Across

1. Ingrid _____ (7)
8. Director of Knocked Up (4,6)
9. Buy your tickets here (3,6)
11. M. Gustave in The Grand Budapest Hotel (7)
12. American Psycho (7,7)
14. Jack Black music teacher (6,2,4)
15. Interview With the _____ (7)
17. Place to put a drink (9)
19. Getaway driver (5)
22. _____ of the Spotless Mind (7,8)
24. Number of people killed in the original Scream (5)
25. Jack Nicholson, Five Easy _____ (6)
28. Star of Star Trek 2009 (5,4)
29. Theme of Stand by Me (10)
30. Glengarry Glen Ross is about four _____ (8)
32. Another word for motion picture (5)
33. Social Network, Eduardo (6,8)
34. Kevin Costner box office bomb (10)
35. 1927's The Jazz Singer was the first _____ (6)
36. Kevin Costner plays a serial killer in Mr. _____ (6)
37. Created Mickey Mouse (6)

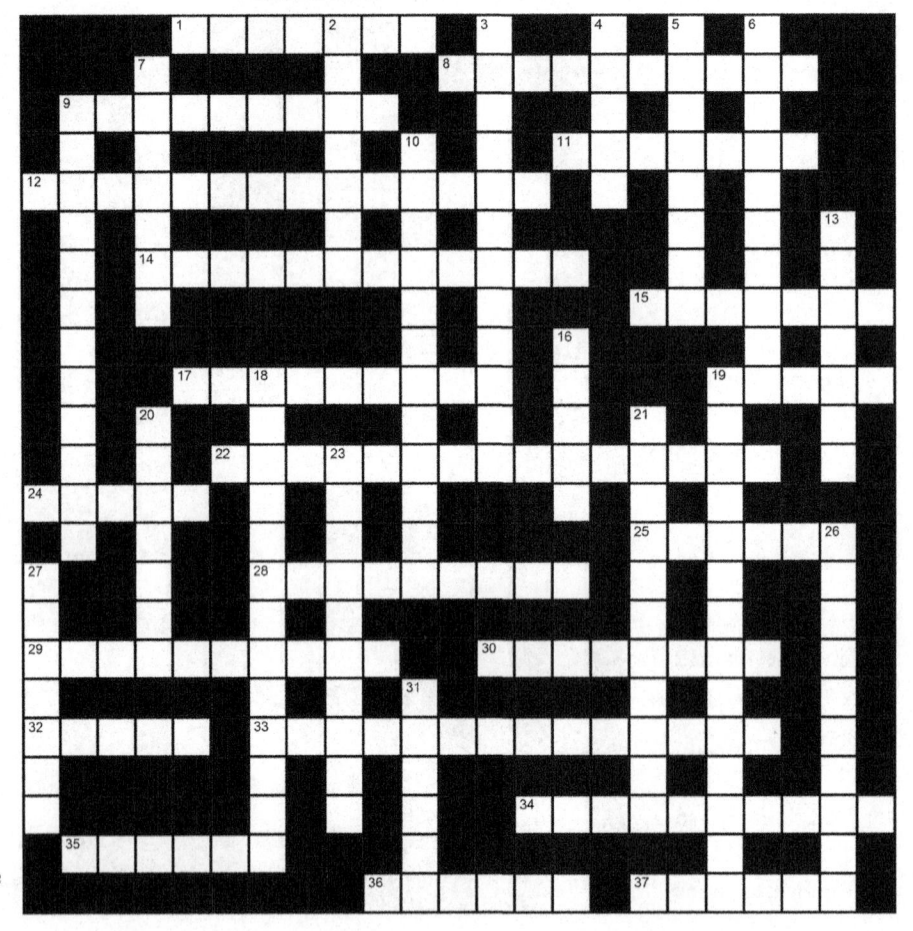

Down

2. Vito's youngest son (7)
3. Star of Pretty Woman (5,7)
4. "We'll always have _____" (5)
5. PTA, Cruise, Hoffman, Julianne Moore, Frogs (8)
6. Texas Chainsaw Massacre director (4,6)
7. The Sugarland _____ (7)
9. Highest grossing movie 2018, Marvel (5,7)
10. Town in It's a Wonderful Life (7,5)
13. Linguist tries to communicate with aliens (7)
16. Robert Shaw's character in Jaws (5)
18. Star of Ghost (7,6)
19. Won best actor in 1989 for My Left Foot (6,3,5)
20. Eastwood plays an 80 year old drug runner (3,4)
21. 2 rival magicians, Bale, Jackman (3,8)
23. Hitchcock, wheelchair (4,6)
26. The script of the film (10)
27. Dustin _____ (7)
31. Sigourney _____ (6)

#33

Across

1. Stars in Pearl (2022) (3,4)
6. Ashley Judd and Tommy Lee, can't be charged twice (6,8)
8. McConaughey character in Interstellar (6)
11. Shown before the main feature (8)
12. The Skin I ___ (4,2)
13. The Banshees of _____ (9)
16. Scarlett Johansson Marvel (5,5)
17. Used technology to make DeNiro look young, The _____ (8)
18. Won best actress in 1967 for Guess Who's Coming to Dinner (9,7)
20. Villain in Harry Potter (9)
24. Isabelle _____ (7)
25. Back to the Future, Marty (5)
26. Plays Indiana Jones (8,4)
27. Star of Inception (8)
30. Star of The Jerk (5,6)
33. Will Turner in Pirates of the Caribbean (7,5)
34. Edge of _____ (8)
35. Eastwood, Escape from _____ (8)
36. Point Break director, Kathryn (7)

Down

1. To Kill a _____ (11)
2. _____ Kings (5)
3. Colonel in Apocalypse Now (5)
4. Brad Pitt, Fight Club (5,6)
5. Ghost removal service (12)
6. High schooler sees visions of a man in a bunny suit (6,5)
7. 1984, Once Upon a Time in _____ (7)
9. Played the villain in Speed (6,6)
10. Mike Myers spy comedies (6,6)
14. King Kong 2005 director, Peter _____ (7)
15. Her head was in the box (7,7)
19. Skyscraper in Die Hard (8,5)
21. Slumdog _____ (10)
22. Wesley Snipes vampire (5)
23. Oscar Isaac gambling movie (4,7)
28. Clooney, Michael _____ (7)
29. Won best actor in 1936 The Story of Louis Pasteur (4,4)
31. Series of short clips combined into one sequence (7)
32. A _____ Under the Influence (5)

#34

Across

1. The Squid and the _____ (5)
2. Wakanda Forever (5,7)
6. Number of dwarfs (5)
7. Movie theater with many different screens (9)
9. Highest grossing movie of 1986, sequel released in 2022 (3,3)
10. Bruce Willis, The Last Boy _____ (5)
13. Kong:_____ (5,6)
15. Star of Donnie Darko (4,10)
18. Number of Austin Powers movie (5)
19. Played Nixon in the 1995 movie Nixon (7,7)
23. The King of Comedy star (2,4)
24. The Usual _____ (8)
27. Won best actress in 1996 for Fargo (7,9)
29. Director Jane ____ (7)
30. Highest grossing movie of 2007, 3rd movie in the franchise (6,3)
31. Don't Worry _____ (7)
32. Taxi Driver city (3,4)
33. Billy Bob, Sling _____ (5)
34. Hakuna Matata (2,7)
35. Man in large rabbit suit (6,5)
36. Robert Redford baseball movie (3,7)
37. Won best actor in 1941 Sergeant York, Gary _____ (6)

Down

1. Breaking the _____, von Trier (5)
3. 2000, Bret Easton Ellis (8,6)
4. Gross Pointe Blank is about a (6)
5. Little Miss _____ (8)
8. Roman ____ (8)
11. Actor who plays Doctor Zhivago (4,6)
12. Charlize ____ (6)
14. Oscar winner, Forest _____ (8)
16. Jack Nicholson's team (6)
17. Won best actress in 1933 for Morning Glory (9,7)
20. Call Me By ____ (4,4)
21. Won best actor in 1966 for A Man for All Seasons (4,8)
22. 1964 James Bond (10)
25. "Made it, Ma! Top of the _____!" (5)
26. Won best actress in 1998 for Shakespeare in Love (7)
28. Highest grossing movie of 1990, Christmas (4,5)
29. Dragged Across _____, Mel Gibson, Vince Vaughn (8)
30. Kingsman: The Secret _____ (7)

#35

Across

1. Won best actress in 2015 for Room (4,6)
5. Highest grossing movie 2011, based on book (5,6)
7. Johnny Depp, Sleepy _____ (6)
8. Risky Business actor (3,6)
9. Movie about a killer car, Stephen King (9)
10. Star of Spider Man No Way Home (3,7)
14. There are this many Godfather movies (5)
15. Django _____ (9)
16. Guess Who's Coming to _____ (6)
20. Costner and Connery movie about Al Capone, The _____ (12)
21. Vertigo takes place in this city (3,9)
26. In Jurassic Park the dino DNA was discovered from a _____ (8)
27. 500 Days of _____ (6)
28. Director of Network and 12 Angry Men (6,5)
31. Star of Grease (4,8)
32. _____ and Ebert (6)
33. 7 sequels and a tv show, comedy (6,7)
34. Plays a PUA in Magnolia (6)
35. Ghost in the _____ (5)
36. Leave Her to _____ (6)

Down

1. Ferris (7)
2. 1989 Indiana Jones, _____ (4,7)
3. Narration by unseen speaker (5,4)
4. Hugh Jackman's daughter goes missing (9)
5. Burt Reynolds plays a stuntman 1978 (6)
6. Director of Beau Travail (6,5)
9. "Mama always said life was like a box of _____" (10)
11. Brokeback _____ (8)
12. Set in SF, Hitchcock, James Stewart (7)
13. Star of The Truman Show (3,6)
17. Won best actress in 1941 for Suspicion (4,8)
18. Hannah and ____ (3,7)
19. Ingmar (7)
22. Norma Desmond's pet in Sunset Boulevard (10)
23. Sex, Lies, and _____ (9)
24. Chinatown city (3,7)
25. Bill Murray's job in Groundhog Day (10)
29. Incorrectly announced as the winner of best picture, 2017 (2,2,4)
30. Won best actor in 1980 for Raging Bull (2,4)

#36

Across

2. Meg Ryan's username in You've Got Mail (8)
6. Meet the Parents, Ben Stiller's character (4,6)
9. Ex _____ (7)
11. Voice of donkey in Shrek (5,6)
13. Won best actor in 1976 for Network (5,5)
14. Won best actor for The King's Speech in 2010 (5,5)
15. Won best actor in 1978 for Coming Home (3,6)
17. BJ Novak 2022 comedy/mystery (9)
19. Won best actor in 1958 for Separate Tables (5,5)
22. "Who's on _____" (5)
23. Won best actress in 1986 for Children of a Lesser God (6,6)
26. One Hundred and One _____ (10)
32. 2018 Neil Armstrong movie (5,3)
34. Coal Miner's _____ (8)
35. Washed-up superhero (7)
36. Nicolas Cage ambulance driver, Bringing Out _____ (3,4)
37. Won best actress in 1959 for Room at the Top (6,8)
38. Wife fakes own death (4,4)

Down

1. Won best actress in 1957 for The Three Faces of Eve (6,8)
3. Won best actress in 1997 for As Good as It Gets (5,4)
4. Person who finances movie (8)
5. Director and actor, Charlie _____ (7)
7. Subject Robin Williams teaches in Dead Poets Society (7)
8. Mississippi _____ (7)
10. Francis Ford _____ (7)
12. One Upon a Time in _____ (3,4)
16. Scorsese movie set in Boston (3,8)
18. Howard Beale anchorman (7)
19. Dumb and _____ (6)
20. Director of Zodiac (5,7)
21. Won best actress in 1980 for portayal of Loretta Lynn (5,6)
24. Ryan Gosling musical (2,2,4)
25. Mini Me, Austin Powers (5,6)
27. Michael Bay space movie, Bruce Willis, Ben Affleck (10)
28. Stand-in for actor that does dangerous scenes (5,3)
29. Aubrey Plaza, Emily the _____ (8)
30. James Cameron water movie 1989, Ed Harris (3,5)
31. Recurring Charlie Chaplin character (3,5)
33. An outdoor movie theater (5,2)

#37

Across

2. Won best actress in in 1999 for Boys Don't Cry (6,5)
7. The Shell With Shoes On (6)
9. Unedited footage from each day (7)
12. Silver Linings _____ (8)
13. A History of _____ (8)
15. Won best actress in 2020 for Nomadland, _____ McDormand (7)
16. Shirley ____ (8)
17. Won best actress in 1932 for The Sin of Madelon Claudet (5,5)
18. The Shawshank Redemption based on the book by (7,4)
21. Man Of Steel star (5,6)
22. Hermione _____ (7)
26. Synonym for film industry (9)
30. Batman Returns holiday (9)
32. Lawyer, Erin ____ (10)
33. Woody in Toy Story is a ____ (6)
34. Star of High Fidelity (4,6)
35. Translation of foreign dialogue on screen (8)
36. Director, Ridley _____ (5)
37. Hulk alter ego (5,6)

Down

1. Nominated a record 17 times (5,6)
3. De Niro character in Casino (3,9)
4. Lord of Rings filmed here (3,7)
5. Played the Joker in the Dark Knight (5,6)
6. A Beautiful Mind is based on the real life of this man (4,4)
8. Pan's _____ (9)
10. Won best actor in 1969 for True Grit (4,5)
11. The Hangover, Zach _____ (12)
14. Won best actor in 1990 for Reversal of Fortune (6,5)
19. Wonder Woman (3,5)
20. Won best actor in 1973 for Save the Tiger (4,6)
23. Redford's character in The Natural (3,5)
24. Won best actress in 1993 for The Piano (5,6)
25. Invisible tall rabbit (6)
27. Mr. Smith Goes to _____ (10)
28. Horror director, John ____ (9)
29. The Virgin _____ (8)
31. Richard Dreyfuss' character in Jaws (6)

#38

Across

3. Director of Face/Off (4,3)
6. A fog traps a town in a grocery store (3,4)
10. Captain America: The _____ _____ (6,7)
12. 12 Angry Men city (3,4)
13. Star of Natural Born Killers (9)
16. The Rock DC Movie (5,4)
18. Wedding _____ (8)
21. Transformers director (7,3)
22. Three Billboards Outside Ebbing, _____ (8)
25. High school students meet in detention (9,4)
26. The Slumber Party _____ (8)
27. Life finds a way. (8,4)
29. Research team in Antarctica is attacked by a shape shifting creature (3,5)
31. Inglourious _____ (8)
32. Another name for a celebrity (5,4)
33. Won best actor in 1967 for In the Heat of the Night (3,7)
34. Won best actress in 1958 for I Want to Live! (5,7)

Down

1. Film industry (7)
2. Henry: Portrait of a Serial _____ (6)
3. Director of The Searchers (4,4)
4. Michael Douglas plays an English professor (6,4)
5. Raiders of the _____ (4,3)
7. Director Werner _____ (6)
8. Won Oscar for best actor, The Father (7)
9. Voice of Gill in Finding Nemo (6,5)
11. Dances with _____ (6)
14. The Hunt for _____, Jack Ryan (3,7)
15. William Hurt and Albert Brooks cable news (9,4)
17. Jack Nicholson plays a retired insurance salesman (5,7)
19. A big hit (11)
20. The Great _____, Chaplin (8)
21. McCabe & Mrs. _____ (6)
23. Alec _____ (7)
24. Star of the "Before" trilogy (5,5)
27. Hugh _____, Wolverine (7)
28. Internal _____ (7)
30. Head electrician on movie set (6)

#39

Across

1. "When you deal a fast shuffle, love is in the cards." (3,4,3)
3. Cinderella's stepsisters, Anastasia and _____ (8)
7. _____ and _____ in Las Vegas (4,8)
8. Won best actress in 1995 for Dead Man Walking (8)
11. Charlie and the Chocolate _____ (7)
12. _____, the Wrath of God (7)
13. The Deer _____ (6)
14. Story of Henry Hill (10)
16. Won best actor for Crazy Heart in 2009 (4,7)
19. Won best actress in 1984 for Places in the Heart (5,5)
21. Star of Rear Window (5,7)
25. Michael Douglas has had enough (7,4)
26. Fast and the _____ (7)
27. Won best actress in 1935 for Dangerous (5,5)
28. Zach Snyder movie that was made into an HBO miniseries (8)
31. Star of Night at the Museum (3,7)
32. M. Night (9)
33. Star Wars director (6,5)
34. Tootsie kickstarted her career (5,5)
35. Animated films (8)
36. Suspenseful adventure story (8)

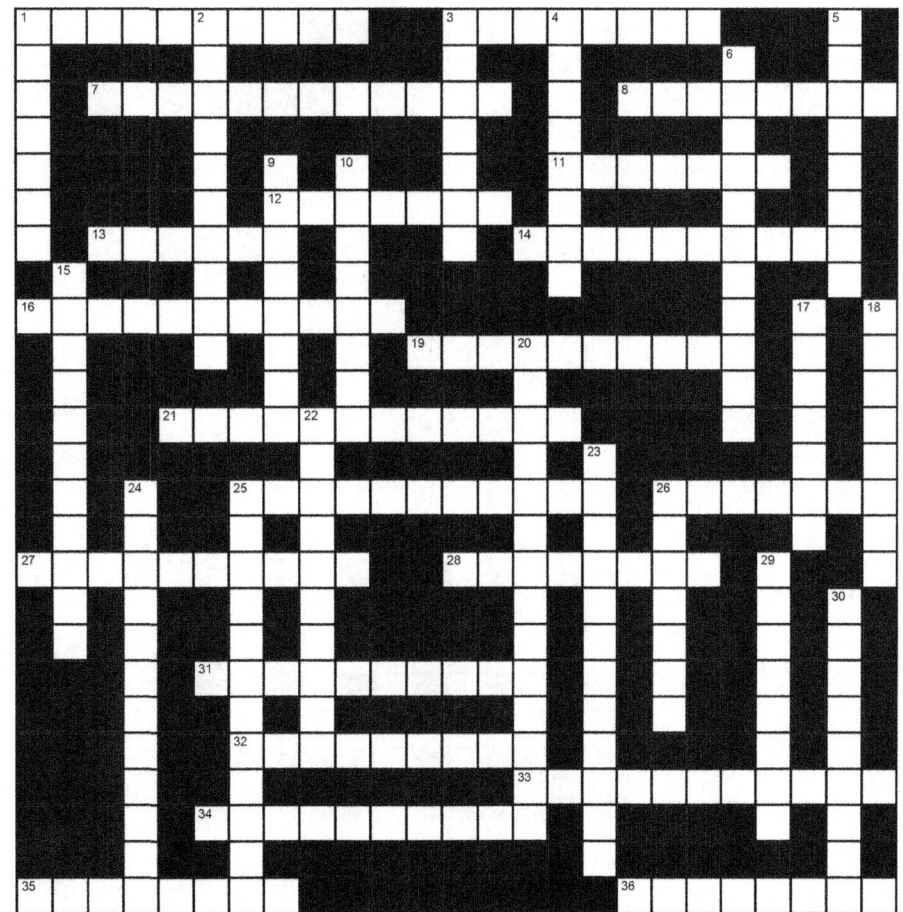

Down

1. Plays Mr. Orange in Reservoir Dogs (3,4)
2. Mark Ruffalo exposes company (4,6)
3. Civilian boats rescue soldiers during World War II (7)
4. Star of 17 Again (3,5)
5. Teenage girl possessed, mother seeks the help of two priests (8)
6. 1975 Kubrick, Ryan O'Neal (5,6)
9. Clooney and Roberts, Ticket to ____ (8)
10. "Round up the usual _____" (8)
15. Won best actress in 1982 for Sophie's Choice (5,6)
17. Cat on a Hot _____ (3,4)
18. Director of Chinatown (8)
20. "My precious." (4,2,3,5)
22. Tinker Tailor _____ _____ (7,3)
23. Robin Williams is a lonely photo guy (3,4,5)
24. Wilson brothers, Wes Anderson, 1996 (6,6)
25. The Bride of _____ (12)
26. Ryan Reynolds is a video game character (4,3)
29. Jackie Chan and Chris Tucker (4,4)
30. Michael Bay 2022 movie (9)

#40

Across

3 Won best actress in 1940 for Kitty Foyle (6,6)
7 Portayed Hannibal Lecter 5 years before Anthony Hopkins (5,3)
8 Won best actress in 1945 for Mildred Pierce (4,8)
9 17 Again, sport (10)
10 Highest grossing movie 2010, 3rd movie in the franchise (3,5)
13 Butch and Sundance are _____ (7)
15 Highest grossing movie of 1994 (7,4)
18 Children of Men star (5,4)
21 Firefighter Kurt Russell movie (9)
26 The _____ Candidate (10)
27 Val ____ (6)
28 Mean Girls villain (6,6)
29 London gangster Jack Carter (3,6)
32 Star of The French Connection (7)
33 2000 Oscar-winning movie set in ancient Rome (9)
34 Butch Cassidy and the _____ (8,3)
35 Pulp _____ (7)
36 De Palma, Phantom of the _____ (8)
37 Director of M, German (5,4)

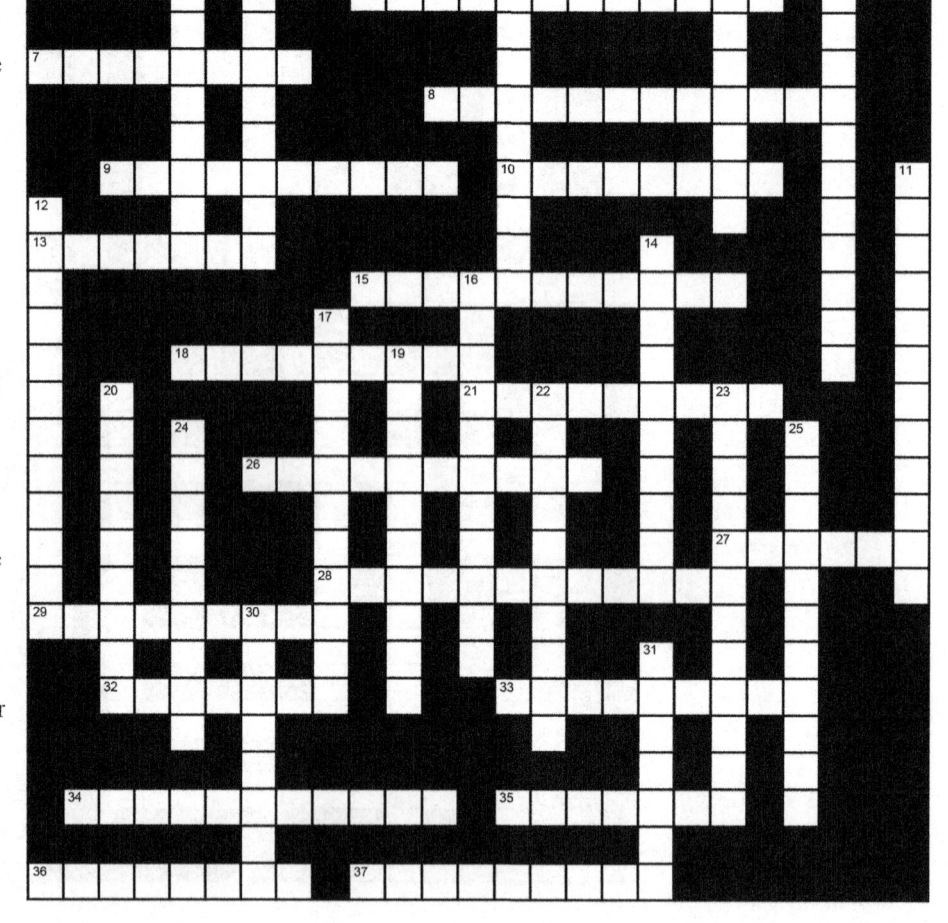

Down

1 Animations set to classical music (8)
2 Hackman basketball coach (8)
4 Plays Gosling love interest in Crazy, Stupid, Love (4,5)
5 Star of The Natural (7)
6 Michael Douglas character in Wall Street (6,5)
11 Won best actress in 1929 for Coquette (4,8)
12 Won best actress in 1947 for The Farmer's Daughter (7,5)
14 Won best actor in 1956 for The King and I (3,7)
16 Anchorman (3,8)
17 Won best actress in 2006 for The Queen (5,6)
19 Where is Mr. Smith going? (10)
20 Sport they play in Harry Potter (9)
22 Won best actor in 1934 It Happened One Night (5,5)
23 Doctor creates a human monster (12)
24 Star of Memento (3,6)
25 Star of Anchorman (4,7)
30 Won best actor in 1994 for Forrest Gump (3,5)
31 _____ Neverland (7)

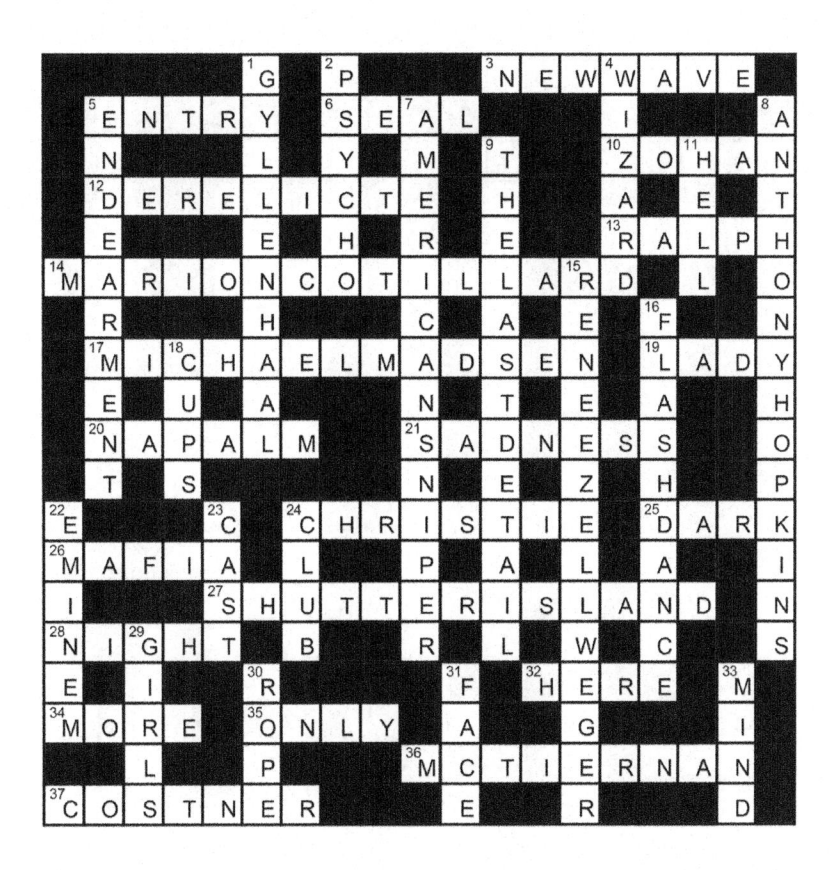

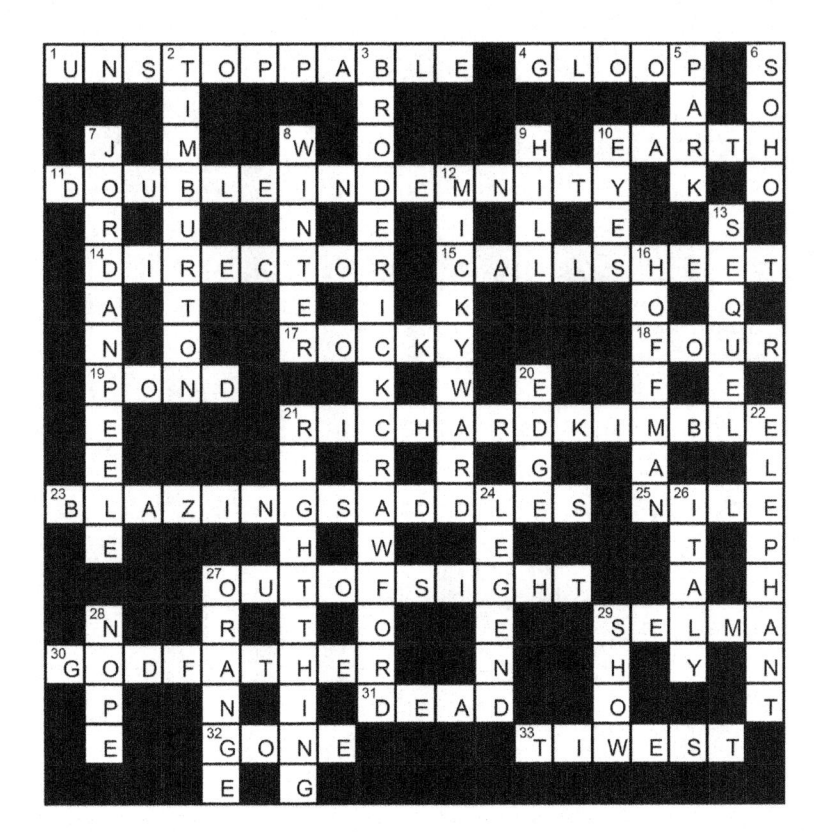

1

2

3

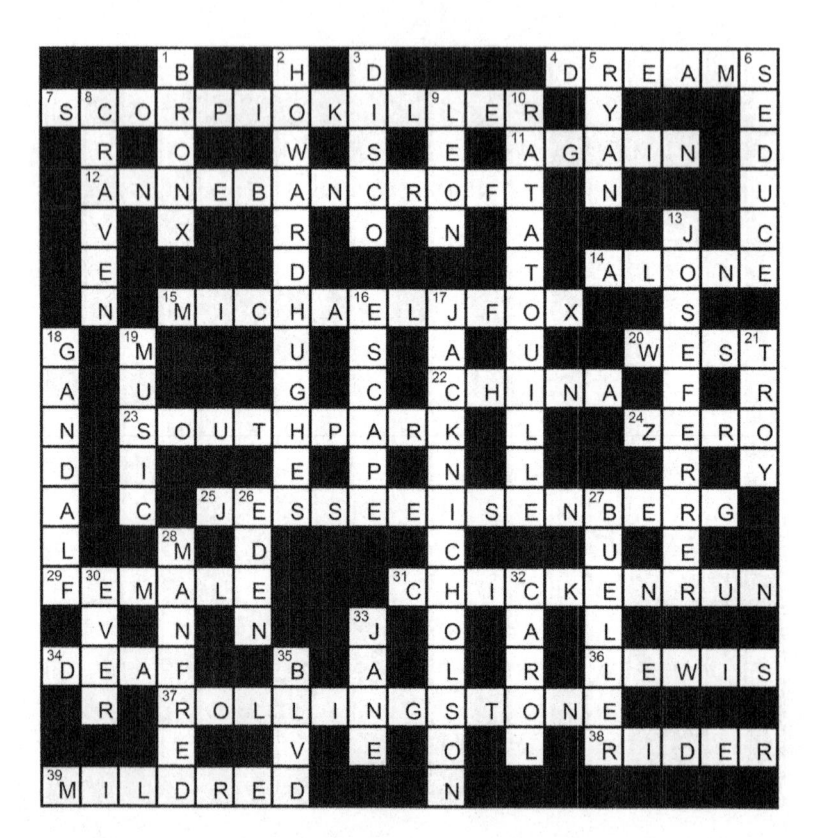

	S	T	R	I	K	E	S	B	A	C	K		H	U	G	O		P
		H		N			A		R		I							R
B	E	A	S	T		T	R	A	D	I	N	G	P	L	A	C	E	S
		N		O			D		S		H		I					J
W	O	R	M	H	O	L	E		T		F		N					U
	R			N				M	A	V	E	R	I	C	K			D
	T			I					N		L		A					I
	H			A		A		G		B		E				R		C
	P				L	O	U	I	S	E	F	L	E	T	C	H	E	R
R	O	O	M			M		C		L		I		E		O		
	L					O		C	O	L	L	A	T	E	R	A	L	
L	E	B	O	W	S	K	I			E						K		F
		E				T			B	O	A	T		W				
O		R				F				N		S	I	M	P	L	E	
F	A	R	Q	U	A	A	D		A		C			N		R		S
J		Y		M		E	R			G	O	O	D			A		I
U			Y	O	U	R	E	D	E	A	D					D		
L	E	O	N			U	E		O		M	A	R	Y	L	A	N	D
Y			S				K		E									E

4

				B		H		D		D	R	E	A	M	S
S	C	O	R	P	I	O	K	I	L	L	E	R		Y		E
	R		O		W		S		E		A	G	A	I	N	D
A	N	N	E	B	A	N	C	R	O	F	T		N			U
	V		X		R		O		N		A		J			C
	E		D				T		A	L	O	N	E			E
	N		M	I	C	H	A	E	L	J	F	O	X		S
G	M		U		S		A		U		W	E	S	T
A	U		G		C	H	I	N	A		F		R
N	S	O	U	T	H	P	A	R	K		Z	E	R	O
D	I		E		P		L			R			Y
A	C	J	E	S	S	E	E	I	S	E	N	B	E	R	G
L	M		D				C			U		E
F	E	M	A	L	E		C	H	I	C	K	E	N	R	U	N
V	N		J	O	A	L
D	E	A	F	B	A	L	R	L	E	W	I	S
R	R	O	L	L	I	N	G	S	T	O	N	E
E	V	E	O	R	I	D	E	R
M	I	L	D	R	E	D

5

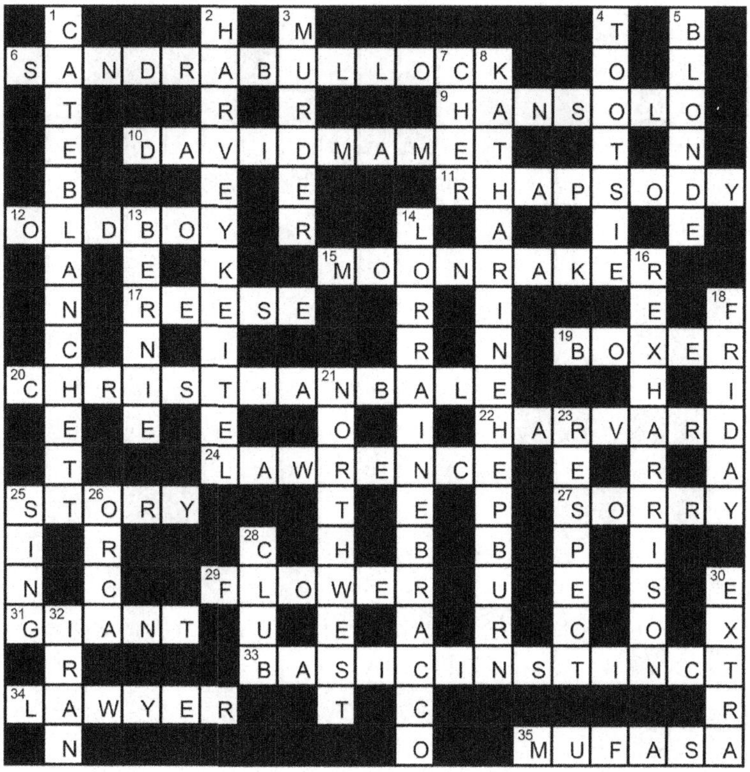

6 SANDRABULLOCK
9 HANSOLO
10 DAVIDMAMET
11 RHAPSODY
12 OLDBOY
15 MOONRAKER
17 REESE
19 BOXER
20 CHRISTIANBALE
22 HARVARD
24 LAWRENCE
25 STORY
27 SORRY
29 FLOWER
31 GIANT
33 BASICINSTINCT
34 LAWYER
35 MUFASA

6

1 DREAM
3 CUBA
5 ARGO
11 INGRIDBERGMAN
14 ELLEN
15 PETDETECTIVE
17 PAULLUKAS
19 MALEFICENT
23 HEAT
24 BEAUTIFUL
25 LATER
26 TRUTH
28 EYESWIDESHUT
30 DAWN
32 BLANK
33 AUDREYHEPBURN
34 DAFOE
35 SHAME

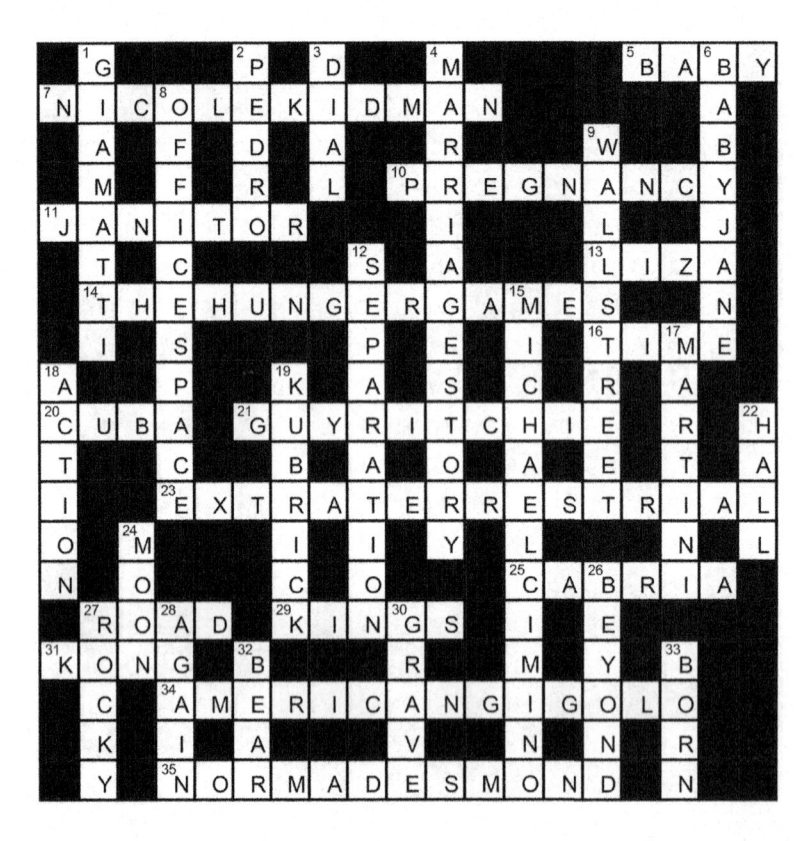

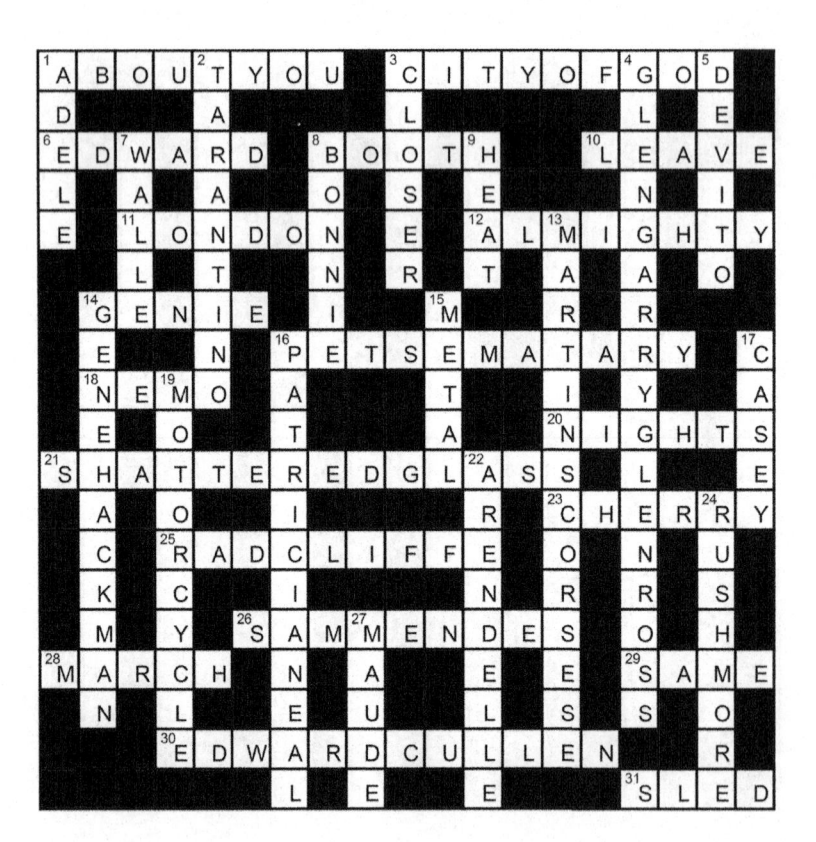

7

	1 G				2 P		3 D			4 M					5 B	A	6 B	Y
7 N	I	C	8 O	L	E	K	I	D	M	A	N						A	
	A		F		D		A			R				9 W			B	
	M		F		R		L		10 P	R	E	G	N	A	N	C	Y	
11 J	A	N	I	T	O	R				I				L			J	
	T		C					12 S		A				13 L	I	Z	A	
	14 T	H	E	H	U	N	G	E	R	G	A	15 M	E	S			N	
	I		S					P		E		I		16 T	I	17 M	E	
18 A			P			19 K		A		S		C		R		A		
20 C	U	B	A		21 G	U	Y	R	I	T	C	H	I	E		R		22 H
T			C			B		A		O		A		E		T		A
I			23 E	X	T	R	A	T	E	R	R	E	S	T	R	I	A	L
O		24 M				I		I		Y		L				N		L
N		O				C		O				25 C	A	26 B	R	I	A	
	27 R	O	28 A	D		29 K	I	N	30 G	S		I		E				
31 K	O	N	G		32 B				R			M		Y		33 B		
	C		34 A	M	E	R	I	C	A	N	G	I	G	O	L	O		
	K		I		A				V			N		N		R		
	Y		35 N	O	R	M	A	D	E	S	M	O	N	D		N		

8

1 A	B	O	U	2 T	Y	O	U		3 C	I	T	Y	O	F	4 G	O	5 D	
D				A					L						L		E	
6 E	D	7 W	A	R	D		8 B	O	O	T	9 H			10 L	E	A	V	E
L		A		A			O		S		E				N		I	
E		11 L	O	N	D	O	N		E		12 A	L	13 M	I	G	H	T	Y
		L		T			N		R		T		A		A		O	
	14 G	E	N	I	E		I			15 M			R		R			
	E			N		16 P	E	T	S	E	M	A	T	A	R	Y		17 C
	18 N	E	19 M	O		A				T			I		Y			A
	E		O			T				A			20 N	I	G	H	T	S
21 S	H	A	T	T	E	R	E	D	G	L	22 A	S	S		L			E
	A		O			I					R		23 C	H	E	R	24 R	Y
	C		25 R	A	D	C	L	I	F	F	E		O		N		U	
	K		C			I					N		R		R		S	
	M		Y		26 S	A	M	27 M	E	N	D	E	S		O		H	
28 M	A	R	C	H		N		A			E		E		29 S	A	M	E
	N		L			E		U			L		S		S		O	
			30 E	D	W	A	R	D	C	U	L	L	E	N			R	
						L		E			E				31 S	L	E	D

9

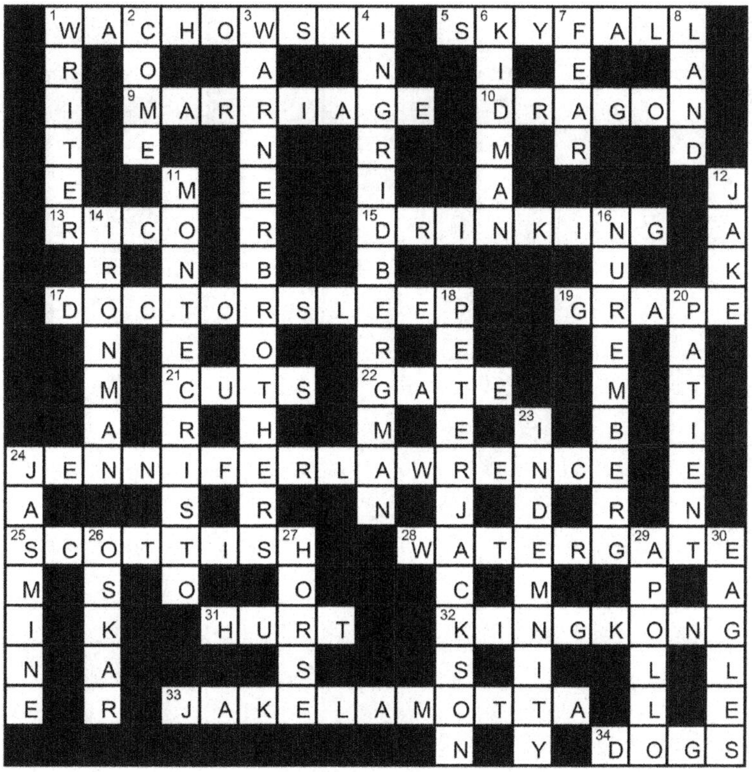
1 WACHOWSKI
5 SKYFALL
9 MARRIAGE
10 DRAGON
13 RICO
15 DRINKING
17 DOCTORSLEEP
19 GRAPE
21 CUTS
22 GATE
24 JENNIFERLAWRENCE
25 SCOTTISH
28 WATERGATE
31 HURT
32 KINGKONG
33 JAKELAMOTTA
34 DOGS

10

1 ASITGETS
5 ROOF
6 APES
10 CRITIC
11 MIND
12 ARIZONA
14 CAMERAMAN
16 PHONEBOOTH
18 SOFIA
20 TIMROBBINS
21 FELIXLEITER
22 REDSOX
24 RONALDCOLMAN
25 LIFE
26 TICKET
28 MAGGIESMITH
31 BADSANTA
32 NATASHA
33 DOCBROWN
34 LEONE
35 TONY

11

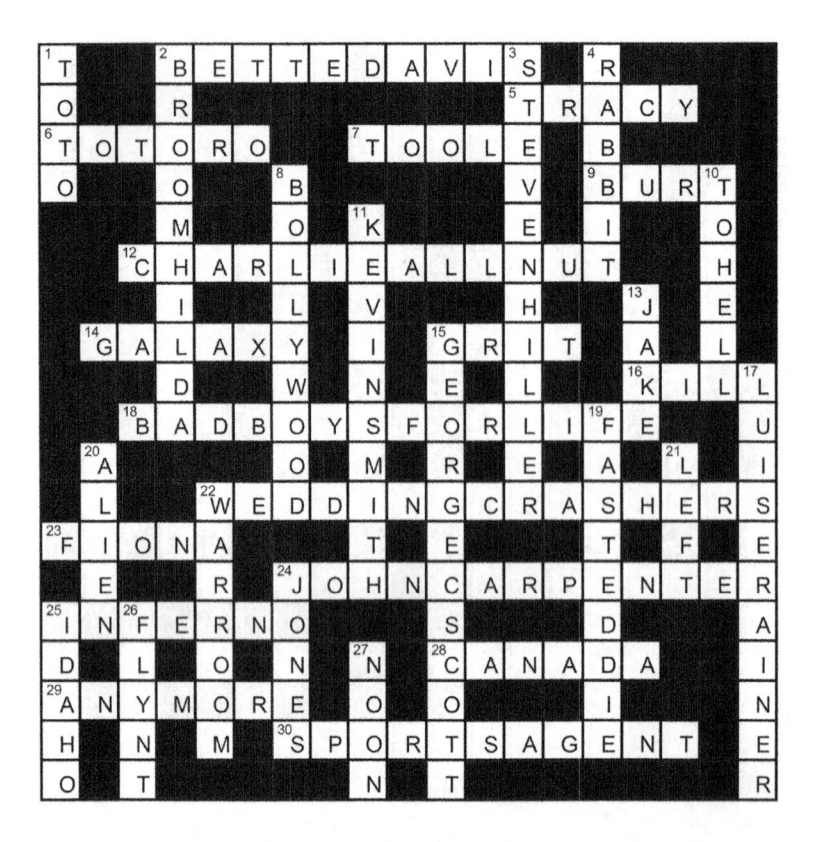

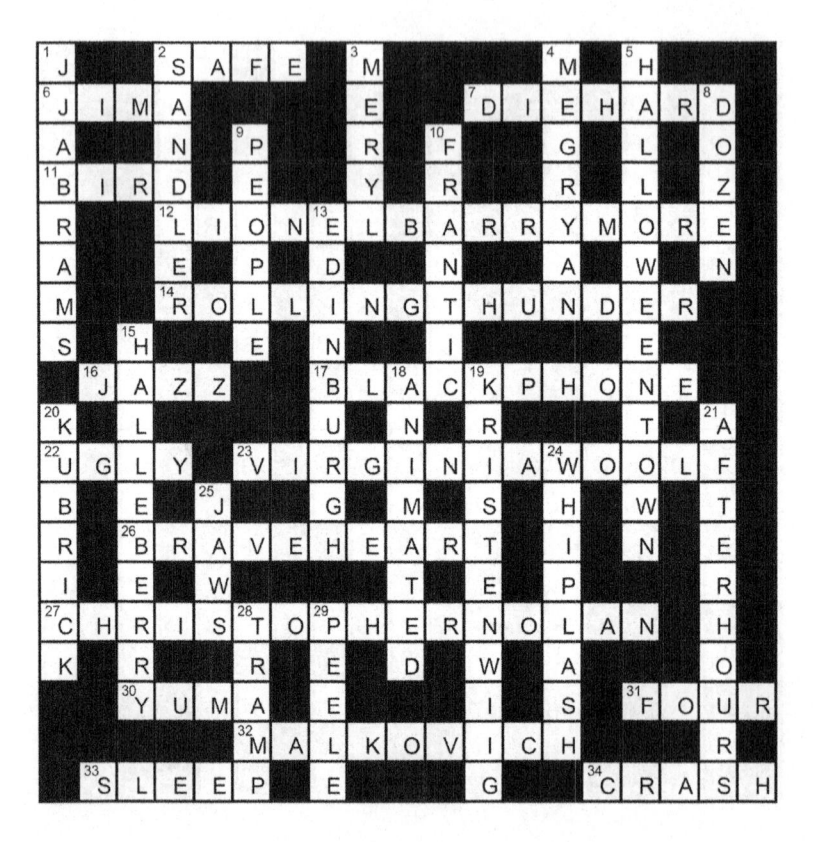

12

13

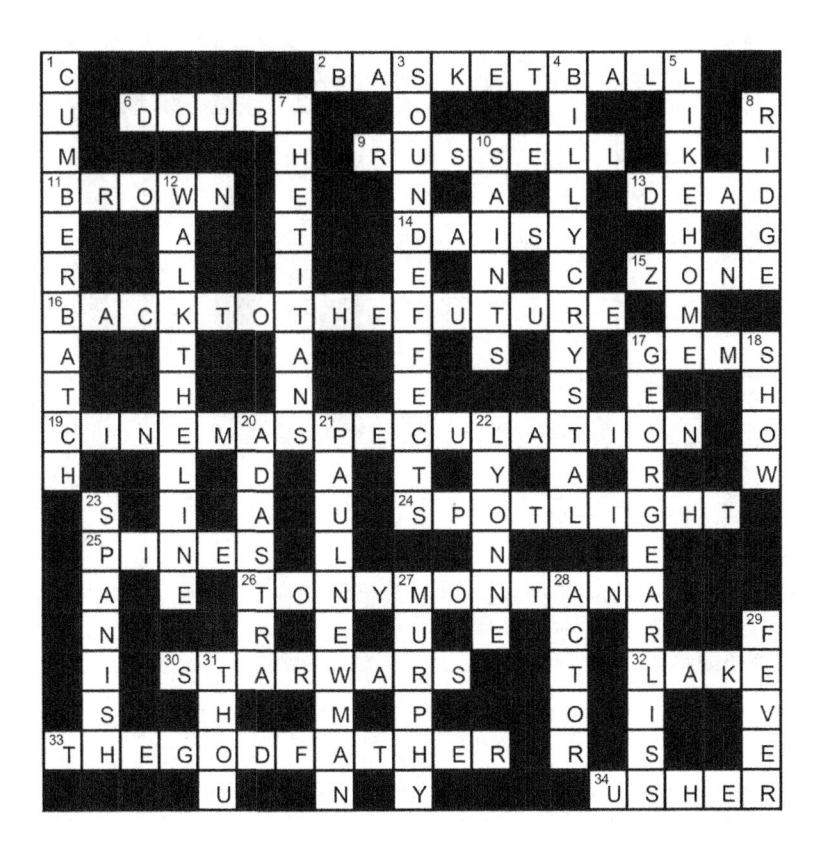

Across:
7. POLTERGEIST
8. MONTYPYTHON
9. CHAPLIN
10. GRYFFINDOR
14. BEATRIXKIDDO
16. OLDMEN
17. TITANIC
19. RED
21. SEVENTEEN
23. WAKANDA
25. TARANTINO
26. WRATH
27. INSIDEOUT
28. LALALAND

Down:
1. INCEPTION
2. STETSON
3. JOHNSON
4. DERTHA (DARTH)
5. VOCOLONE
6. PBARNUM
11. FIND
12. LEON
13. SUPERMAN
14. BILL
15. THXBSA
18. CHOBECCAMA
19. RODCYDINI
20. JUMANJI
22. INDIANA
24. JOKR

14

Across:
2. BASKETBALL
6. DOUBT
9. RUSSELL
11. BROWN
13. DEAD
14. DAISY
15. ZONE
16. BACKTOTHEFUTURE
17. GEM
19. CINEMASPECULATION
24. SPOTLIGHT
25. PINES
26. TONYMONTANA
30. STARWARS
32. LAKE
33. THEGODFATHER
34. USHER

15

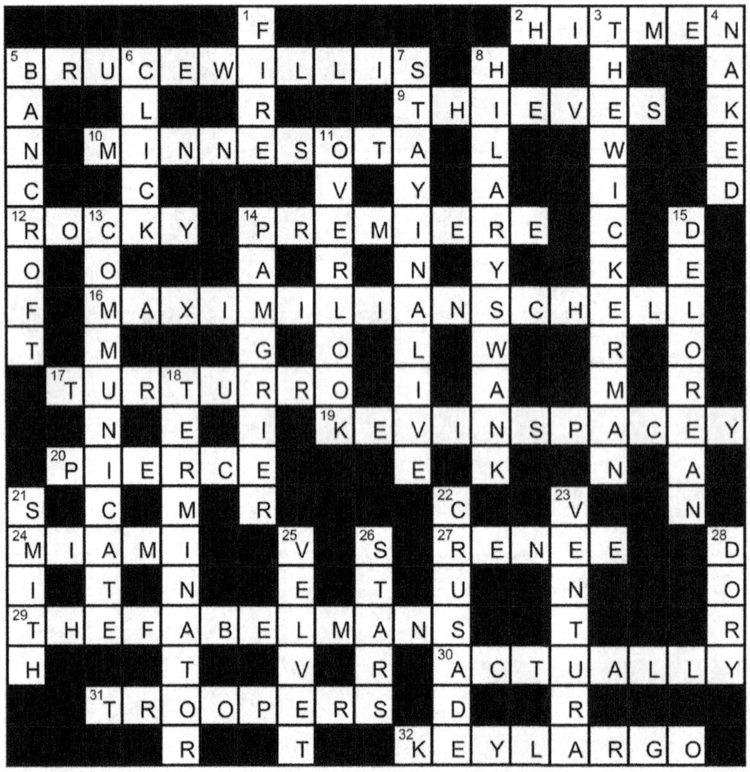

2 HITMEN
5 BRUCEWILLIS
9 THIEVES
10 MINNESOTA
12 ROCKY
14 PREMIERE
16 MAXIMILIANSCHELL
17 TURTURRO
19 KEVINSPACEY
20 PIERCE
24 MIAMI
27 RENEE
29 THEFABELMANS
30 ACTUALLY
31 TROOPERS
32 KEYLARGO

16

2 GREGORYPECK
7 JAWS
10 STREET
11 BOOGIENIGHTS
13 SHAGGED
14 ROBERTALTMAN
16 GREASE
17 DENZELWASHINGTON
22 ROBERTDONAT
25 FRIENDS
26 TYLERPERRY
27 SWINGERS
28 DOGS
29 THESTING
30 FACEBOOK
32 GARYOLDMAN
33 BRANDO

17

19

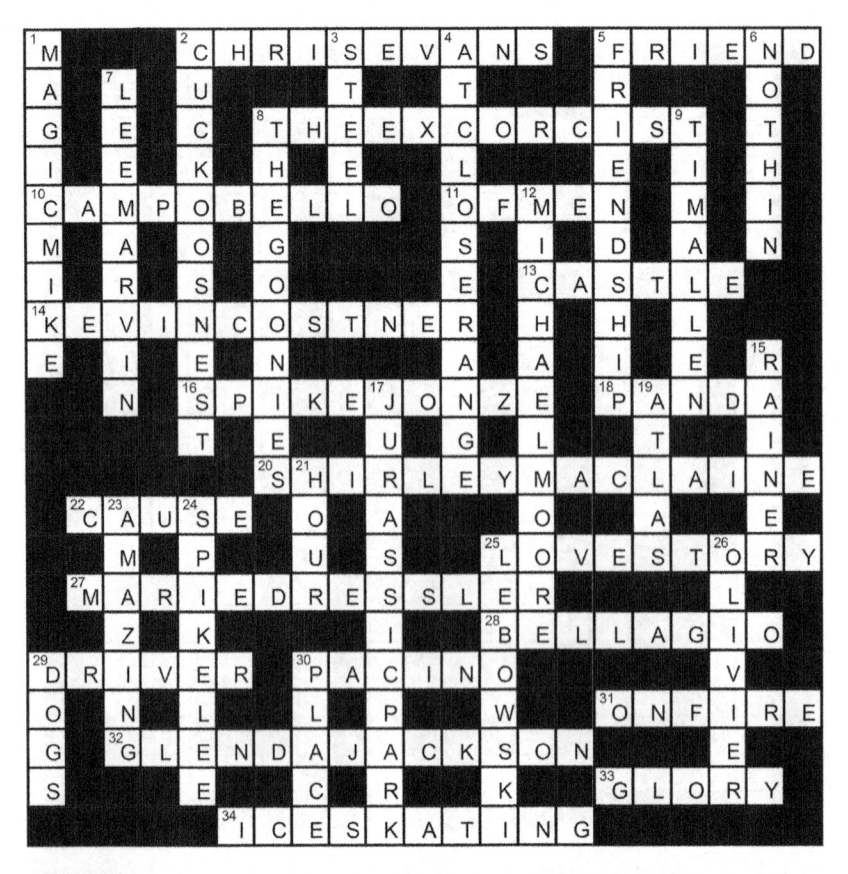

Across:
1. M
2. CHRISEVANS
4. (in 2A)
5. FRIEND
8. THEEXCORCIST
10. CAMPOBELLO
11. OFMEN
13. CASTLE
14. KEVINCOSTNER
15. R
16. SPIKEJONZE
18. PANDA
20/21. SHIRLEYMACLAINE
22. CAUSE
25. LOVESTORY
27. MARIEDRESSLER
28. BELLAGIO
29. DRIVER
30. PACINO
31. ONFIRE
32. GLENDAJACKSON
33. GLORY
34. ICESKATING

20

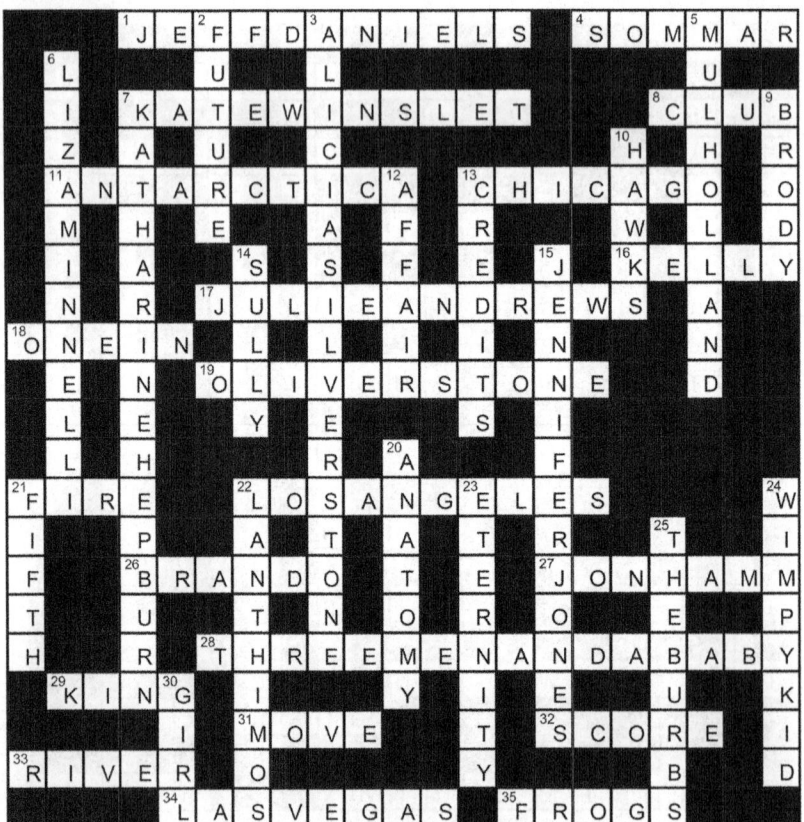

1. JEFFDANIELS
4. SOM
5. MAR
7. KATEWINSLET
8. CLUB
11. ANTARCTICA
13. CHICAGO
16. KELLY
17. JULIEANDREWS
18. ONEIN
19. OLIVERSTONE
21. FIRE
22. LOSANGELES
26. BRANDO
27. JONHAMM
28. THREEMENANDABABY
29. KING
31. MOVE
32. SCORE
33. RIVER
34. LASVEGAS
35. FROGS

21

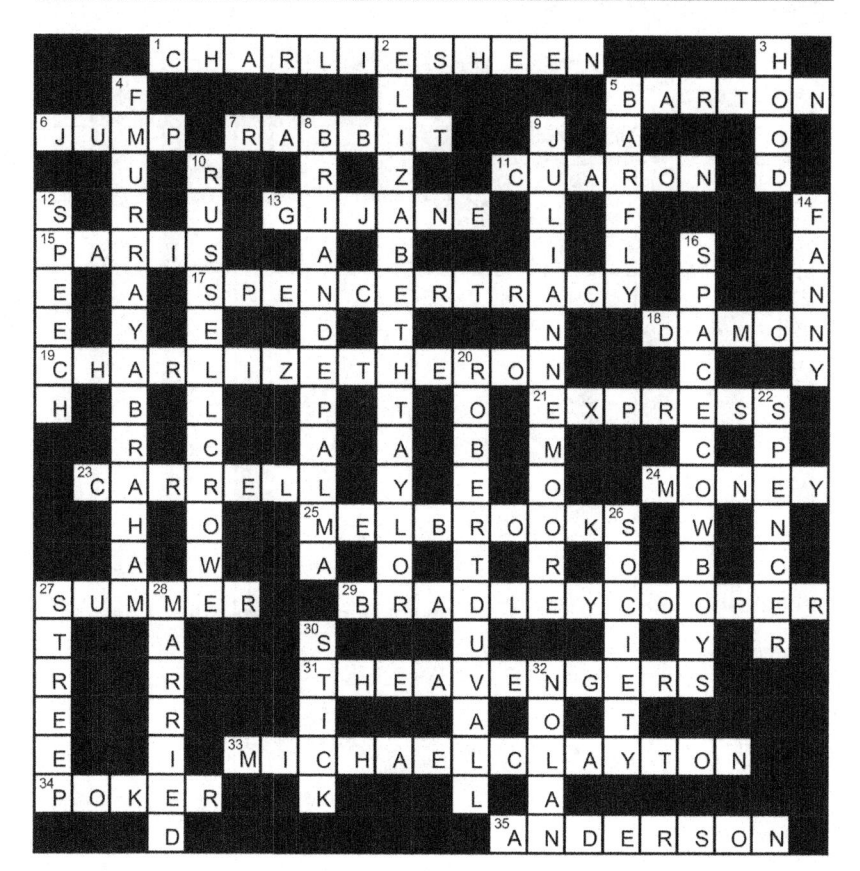

22

23

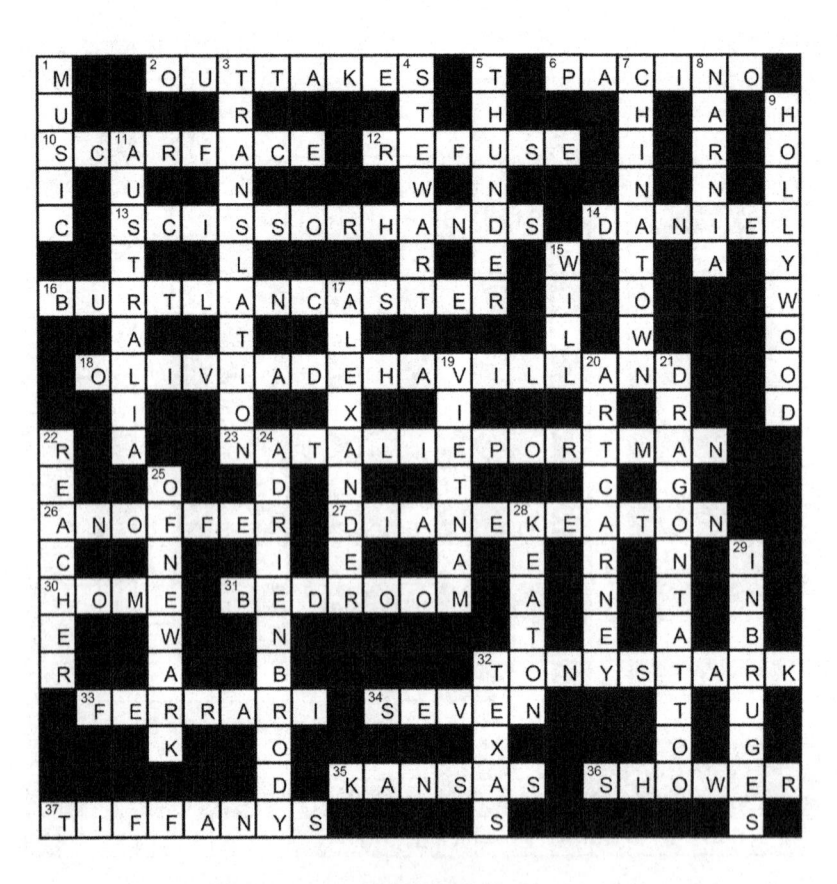

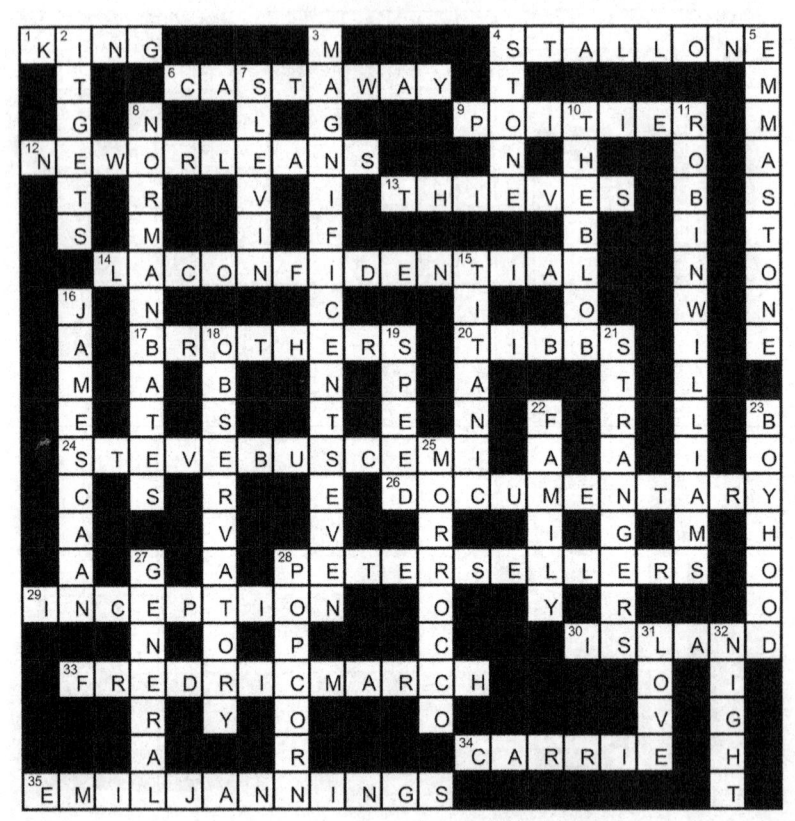

25

26

27

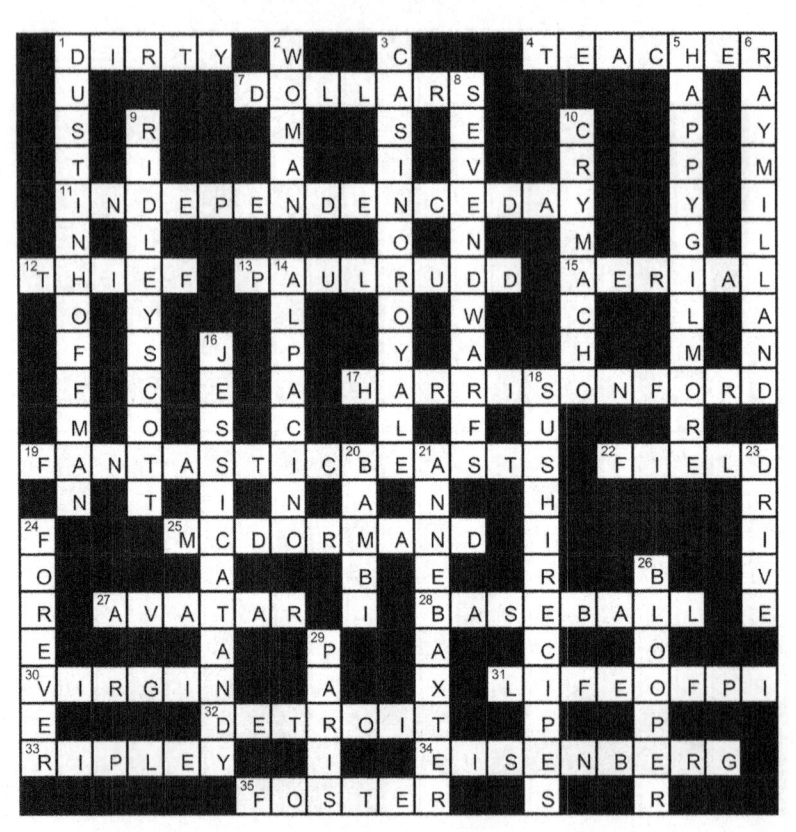

Across and down entries filled in grid:

- LAWYER
- SOPHIALOREN
- MIAFARROW
- SUPERMAN
- JULIAROBERTS
- PURPLE
- PATTINSON
- CHARLTONHESTON
- CROWE
- BUNCH
- TOLKIEN
- SIXTHSENSE
- SMILE
- KEYSER
- MALCOLMX
- JANEWYMAN
- NOSTROMO
- WAVES

Down fills include: GLASSES, PATRONDHOUNDAD, RIDEYPDAY, HAILSTONE, JACKPOT, CHALLOVIX, SCHWEYER, PHYSICIAN, LOVVOVINSON, MOM, CROW, GARAGE, CARR, KINSINS, DONN.

28

- DIRTY
- TEACHER
- DOLLARS
- INDEPENDENCEDAY
- THIEF
- PAULRUDD
- AERIAL
- HARRISONFORD
- FANTASTICBEASTS
- FIELD
- MCDORMAND
- AVATAR
- BASEBALL
- VIRGIN
- LIFEOFPI
- DETROIT
- RIPLEY
- EISENBERG
- FOSTER

Down fills include: DUSTIN, WMA, CSEVER, CAPPY, HARAY, RAYMIL, RILSCO, THOFFM, YSCO, JEEAS, PLACEYAWLFU, ANT, TIN, BEANHIRE, FO, MCA, IN, BBO, PAAXACLP, VERIP, DETROIT, PS, GR.

29

1 COOPER
3 TONYSCOTT
7 PARIS
8 ALASKA
10 MURDER
12 ADAMSANDLER
14 TRAILER
17 JOHNNYCASH
19 DESIRE
22 WILLIAMHOLDEN
23 WATSON
24 CRUISE
25 BILLYBEANE
27 ROBREINER
29 BEBLOOD
31 MCCONAUGHEY
32 MOLLY
33 KEVINGARNETT
34 BANKS

30

1 STUFF
3 MACLACHLAN
8 NICOLASCAGE
9 JANETGAYNOR
10 MIKEMYERS
12 SUSAN
13 PROFESSOR
15 HEREANYMORE
17 JAMESCAMERON
20 SEANCONNERY
21 THEATER
22 STONE
25 MANHUNTER
26 MRJINGLES
27 QUENTINTARANTINO
28 HAROLD
29 ROBERTDENIRO
30 THEBIGSHORT
31 POPPINS
32 POINTBREAK

31

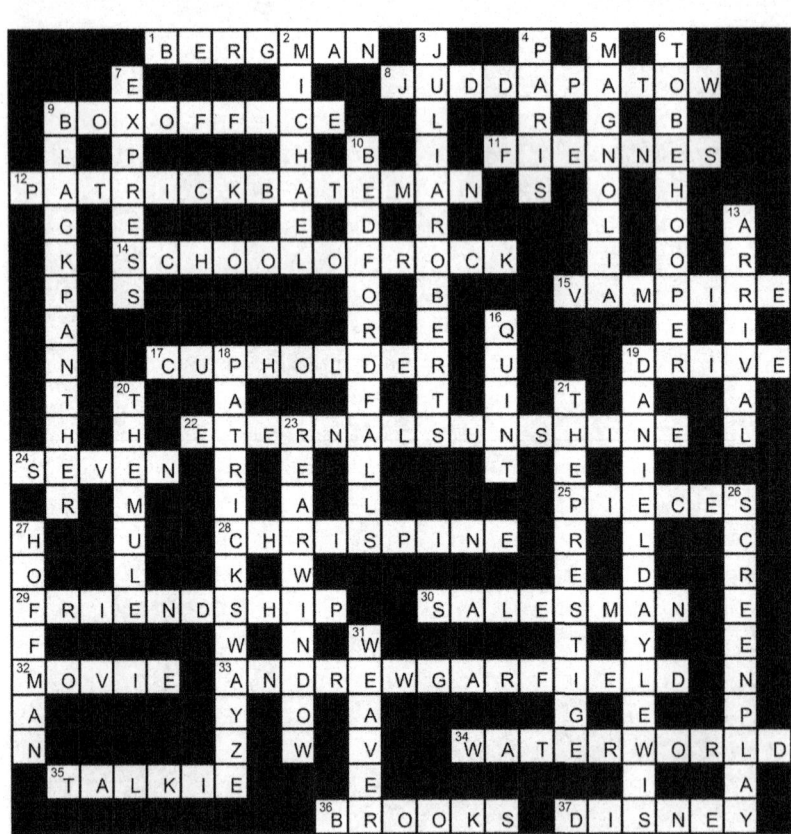

Across/Down answers filled in grid:

W O R L D · B · H E D G E H O G
· R · I · · E · B
J E S S I C A L A N G E · F A R R E L L Y
· A · V · L · H · V · O
S H I R L E Y · M · S · W E D D I N G
M · A · U · C · K · N · D
I · · P H O T O G R A P H E R · S I N C I T Y
T · C · N · R · A · G · E
H · O · T · A · O · M A M A M I A
· D O N T T H E Y · L · E · T · R · M
F · N · E · H · · R I V E R K W A I
L · · J O H N W A T E R S · V · · C
I · R · A · P · E · S · J · H
C · · T · B · A K · P · A · A
K A T H L E E N T U R N E R · I · C · E
· L · · R · R · P · A · N · K · L
· M · R · · F R A N C E S M C D O R M A N D
W O M A N · R · N · E · C · S · O
· D · I · C O M P T O N · R · C L O S E U P
H O U S E · N · H · · H · · G
· V · I · · T R A I N S P O T T I N G
· A · N · E · · · · O · · · L
· R · G · F R E N C H · · · · · S

32

B E R G M A N · J · P · M · T
· · E · I · J U D D A P A T O W
B O X O F F I C E · L · R · G · B
L · P · · B · I · F I E N N E S
P A T R I C K B A T E M A N · S · O · H
C · E · E · D · R · L · O · A
K · · S C H O O L O F R O C K · I · O · R
P · S · · O · B · · V A M P I R E
A · · · · R · E · Q · E · I
N · · C U P H O L D E R · U · D R I V E
T · T · A · F · T · I · T · A · A
H · H · E T E R N A L S U N S H I N E · L
S E V E N · R · E · L · T · E · · ·
· · R · M · I · A · · · · I · · ·
· · · U · A · L · P I E C E S
H · U · C H R I S P I N E · R · L · C
O · L · K · W · · · E · D · R
F R I E N D S H I P · S A L E S M A N · E
F · · · W · N · W · T · Y · · E
M O V I E · A N D R E W G A R F I E L D N
A · · · Y · O · A · · G · E · P
N · · · Z · W · V · W A T E R W O R L D
· T A L K I E · E · · I · A
· · · · B R O O K S · D I S N E Y

33

Across:
1. MIAGOTH
6. DOUBLEJEOPARDY
8. COOPER
11. PREVIEWS
12. LIVEIN
13. INISHERIN
16. BLACKWIDOW
17. IRISHMAN
18. KATHARINEHEPBURN
20. VOLDEMORT
24. HUPPERT
25. MCFLY
26. HARRISONFORD
27. DICAPRIO
30. STEVEMARTIN
33. ORLANDOBLOOM
34. TOMORROW
35. ALCATRAZ
36. BIGELOW

34

Across:
1. WHALE
2. BLACKPANTHER
6. SEVEN
7. MULTIPLEX
9. TOPGUN
10. SCOUT
13. SKULLISLAND
15. JAKEGYLLENHAAL
18. THREE
19. ANTHONYHOPKINS
23. DENIRO
24. SUSPECTS
27. FRANCESMCDORMAND
29. CAMPION
30. SPIDERMAN
31. DARLING
32. NEWYORK
33. BLADE
34. NOWORRIES
35. DONNIEDARKO
36. THENATURAL
37. COOPER

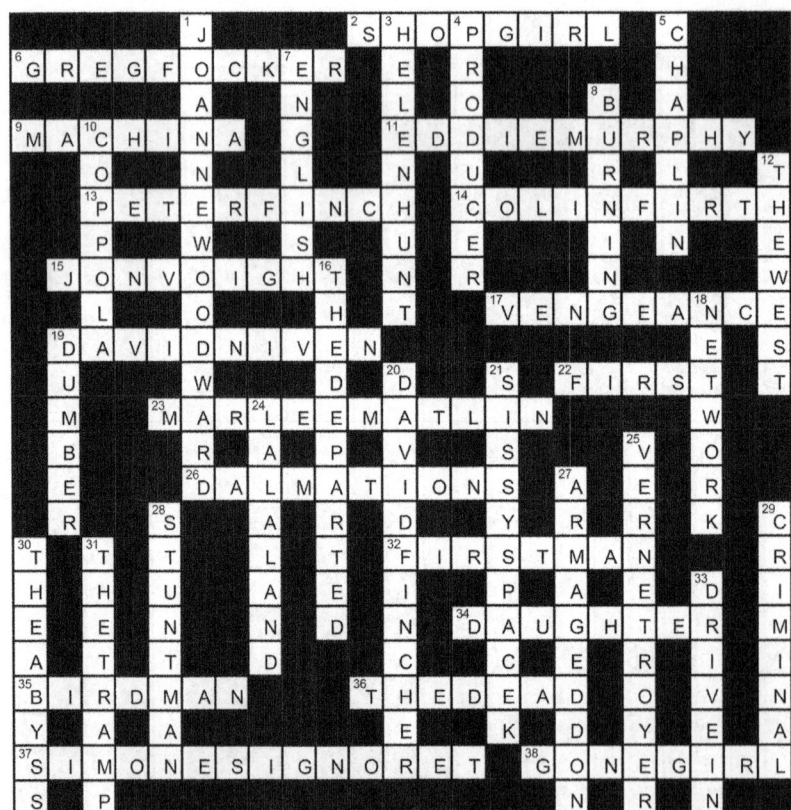

35

36

37

1 MERYLSTREEP
2 HILARYSWANK
3 ACEROTHSTEIN
4 NEWZEALAND
5 HEATHLEDGER
6 JOHNNASH
7 MARCEL
8 LABYRINTH
9 DAILIES
10 JOHNWAYNE
11 GALIFIANAKIS
12 PLAYBOOK
13 VIOLENCE
14 JEREMYIRONS
15 FRANCES
16 MACLAINE
17 HELENHAYES
18 STEPHENKING
19 GALGADOT
20 JACKLEMMON
21 HENRYCAVILL
22 GRANGER
23 ROYHOBBS
24 HOLLYHUNTER
25 HARVEY
26 HOLLYWOOD
27 WASHINGTON
28 CARPENTER
29 SUICIDE
30 CHRISTMAS
31 HOOPER
32 BROCKOVICH
33 COWBOY
34 JOHNCUSACK
35 SUBTITLE
36 SCOTT
37 BRUCEBANNER

38

1 SHOWBIZ
2 KILLER
3 JOHNWOO
3 JOHNFORD
4 WONDERBOY
5 LOSTARK
6 THEMIST
7 HERZOG
8 HOPKINS
9 WILLEMDAFOE
10 WINTERSOLDIER
11 WOLVES
12 NEWYORK
13 HARRELSON
14 REDOCTOBER
15 BROADCASTNEWS
16 BLACKADAM
17 ABOUTSCHMIDT
18 CRASHERS
19 BLOCKBUSTER
20 DICTATOR
21 MICHAELBAY
21 MILLER
22 MISSOURI
23 BALDWIN
24 ETHANHAWK
25 BREAKFASTCLUB
26 MASSACRE
27 JURASSICPARK
27 JACKMAN
28 AFFAIR
29 THETHING
30 GAFFER
31 BASTERDS
32 MOVIESTAR
33 RODSTEIGER
34 SUSANHAYWARD

39

Printed in Great Britain
by Amazon